# *Loving* CATHOLICISM

Viewing Catholicism through the Lens of Love

## Brandy M. Miller

40 Day Writer LLC
Dallas, Texas USA

© 2024 Brandy M. Miller. All rights reserved.

No portion of this book may be reproduced in any form without written permission from the publisher or author, except as permitted by U.S. copyright law.

PERMISSIONS
For permissions, write to:
Permissions c/o 40 Day Writer LLC
2212 Cecille St.
Dallas, TX 75214

DISCLAIMER:
This book is NOT to be taken as official Church teaching. It does NOT have an imprimatur from a local bishop. It has undergone review by two parish priests, but readers are advised to check with their own parish priest to verify the accuracy of the content.

Book Cover by Brandy M. Miller

1st edition 2024

All Scriptures Quoted are from the Knox Bible found on NewAdvent.org.

ISBNs
eBook: 9781948672245
Hardbound: 9781948672221

Printed in the United States of America.

# CONTENTS

Introduction ................................................................... v
Chapter 1. The Need for Love ..................................... 1
Chapter 2. The Limits of Human Love ....................... 5
Chapter 3. The Need for God ...................................... 9
Chapter 4. The holy Trinity of Love .......................... 13
Chapter 5. Finding Love in Heaven, Hell, & Purgatory .... 17
Chapter 6. Humanity's Need for Organized Religion ........ 25
Chapter 7. Choosing the Rght Religion ..................... 31
Chapter 8. Jesus, the Perfect Model of Love ............. 35
Chapter 9. Jesus: Answering Humanity's Greatest Questions about Love .............................................. 39
Chapter 10. The Necessity of the Resurrection ........ 43
Chapter 11. Christ's Parting Gifts: The Holy Spirit and the Catholic Church ................................................ 47
Chapter 12. the Catholic Church: Preserving and Protecting the Truth about Love ............................... 51
Chapter 13. Sacred Tradition: What the Apostles Handed on about Love ............................................... 55
Chapter 14. Sacred Scripture: The Story of God's Love for Humanity ............................................................. 59
Chapter 15. The Sacraments: Equipping Us to Win the Battle for Love ....................................................... 63

Chapter 16. The Pope: Preserving a Perfect Union of Love..................................................................................75

Chapter 17. The Community of Believers: Practicing Love..................................................................................83

Chapter 18. Living in Love: The Laws and the Precepts of the Church..................................................................91

Chapter 19. Celebrating the Mass: Entering Heaven on Earth................................................................................107

Chapter 20. Mary: A Perfect Model of Living for the Sake of Love.......................................................................115

Chapter 21. The Saints: A Great Cloud of Witnesses.....121

Chapter 22. The Rosary: Teaching Us How to Choose Love in Every Circumstance..................................................127

Chapter 23. The Prayers of the Rosary..............................137

Conclusion..............................................................................145

About the Author: Brandy M. Miller......................................149

# INTRODUCTION

This book is an encapsulation of everything I've learned and come to understand about the Catholic Church over the 22 years since my return to the faith. It is my interpretation of the Church's teachings and how I see things. I share it with you that you might see the beauty of the Church the way I do.

## *What the Catholic Church is NOT*

The Catholic Church often carries a bad reputation. So, before we begin, I want to set the record straight. The Catholic Church is not:

- A cult
- Marian worship
- False idolatry

Cults do not encourage questions or free thinking. The Catholic Church encourages both..

*"Beloved, do not believe every spirit, but test the spirits to see whether they are from God, for many false prophets have gone out into the world." – 1 John 4:1*

We'll address more regarding the role of Mary, the Pope, the Saints, and the Rosary in this course. Rest assured that all will be explained and the logic of it is beautiful.

## Welcome! I'm glad you're here

*"There are not one hundred people in the United States who hate the Catholic Church, but there are millions who hate what they wrongly perceive the Catholic Church to be." - Archbishop Fulton J. Sheen*

**Please note: You will see me refer to the Church as a she because Christ refers to the Church as His bride.**

I walked away from the Catholic Church at age 16 because I couldn't find anyone who was Catholic who could answer my questions about why the Catholic Church wanted me to do - or not do - the things she did. I didn't understand my faith and, after being abandoned, abused, and neglected by the adults in my life, I wasn't about to give my blind obedience to anyone.

I assumed that if nobody I knew - including a priest and a sister - could answer my questions, there must not be answers. It never occurred to me to ask God, or this course might not exist. I created this course for all those who:

• Are Catholic and want a deeper understanding of their faith

• Love their Catholic faith and want others to love it, too, but aren't sure how to explain it

• Aren't sure why being Catholic matters or why it's worth the sacrifices required of them

• Are interested in the Catholic faith and want a better understanding of it

If any of that sounds familiar, you are in the right place. Let me share with you a little more about who I am and what makes me qualified to teach you about the Catholic faith.

## About Me

My mother did her best to raise me Catholic but she didn't have a solid understanding of the Catholic faith herself. As I mentioned in the last lesson, I left the Church at age 16. It was shortly before I was supposed to be confirmed into the faith.

I spent the next 12 years doing just about everything the Catholic Church said I shouldn't do. The result? My 7-year-old son standing in my bedroom, looking me in the eyes, telling me not only that he was going to kill himself but exactly how he was going to do it. And he had a backup plan in case that first plan didn't work.

I didn't know what my husband and I did to break this child so badly that death was preferable to life, but I knew we needed to find out . . . and fast! My quest for answers led me to the one place I never expected to go back to - the Catholic Church. In March of 2004, I woke from a dream with God's call to "teach His children how much He loves them."

I didn't know at the time just how unqualified for the job I was, but God doesn't need you to be qualified for the job He asks you to do. He just needs you to be willing to do it.

I've spent the last twenty years studying the Catholic faith and engaging in conversations with atheists, agnostics, nominal Christians, as well as those who are spiritual but not religious, about Christ and the Catholic Church and what we offer the world that no one else can. I want to pass on to you the insights I've gained so that you can access the unconditional love that waits for you in the Catholic Church.

If you're ready to discover how to drink your fill of the living waters of Christ's unconditional love for you - and to understand the consequences that happen when you don't - let's get started.

## *What to Expect*

### Uncover the 'Why' Behind What the Church Does, Teaches, and Expects of Members

I can't give you everything the Church offers in a single course. With over 2,000 years of Catholic history and another 5,000 plus of Jewish history to unpack and unfold, there is no single course that could do that for you. What I am giving you is an overview of the basics so you can see how it all comes back to one thing and one thing only: Helping you to grow in your capacity to give and receive love.

## *This course will provide:*

- Insights into why the Church does what she does, teaches what she teaches, and expects what she expects of her members
- Help in understanding and explaining the Catholic faith to others
- Concrete evidence of man's need for religion and why so many get so little from it
- Explanations of what the Catholic Church offers that no other religion can provide
- An understanding of how Mary, the Pope, and the Saints provide help and support in living out the call to love
- Instruction in how to use the Rosary and its prayers to begin winning the daily battles for love

I want to reassure you of this one thing: Once you understand that helping people learn how to give and receive love is the foundation, purpose, and reason behind everything the Catholic Church does, teaches, preaches, and expects, it all begins to make perfect sense.

## *Exercises*

Journal your answers to the following questions:

1. Who are you?

2. Why are you taking this course?

3. What are you hoping to get from it?

4. What is your experience with the Catholic Church so far?

5. What is the name and city of your nearest Catholic Church?

6. Are you a current member of that parish?

7. If not, do you plan to become one?

8. Why or why not?

## *Let's Pray:*

Lord God, you created us out of love in order to be loved and to give love to those around us. Help us to open up our hearts, our minds, and our lives to you. Help us to see you and to recognize you in all your distressing disguises, as well as in the moments of happiness and plenty. Teach us to walk with you and to know you, that we might be one with you in eternity. We ask all this in the power of the Most Holy and Sacred Name of Our Lord and Savior, Jesus Christ. Amen.

## *What's Next?*

Now that I've set your expectations for what you'll find in this book, let's talk about the human need for love.

# CHAPTER 1. THE NEED FOR LOVE

***You can live without love. But you won't want to.***

*"Psychologists, at least psychologists who write textbooks, not only show no interest in the origin and development of love or affection, but they seem to be unaware of its very existence." - Harry Harlow, The Nature of Love, 1958*

Abraham Maslow fathered the Humanist Movement. His Theory of Human Motivation, published in 1943, is taught in classrooms and educational training programs around the world. It represents the dominant belief system in modern psychology today.

Maslow theorized that all of human behavior is driven by our various needs, but the primary drivers of it all are the bodily needs such as food, water, shelter, and sex. Other needs, such as love and belonging, only come to the forefront once those basic needs are met.

If Maslow were right, America should be the happiest nation in the history of the world. We have more access to food, water, shelter, and sex than any nation in recorded history. Instead, we're the most medicated nation on the planet. Let me share with you the flaws that Harry Harlow uncovered in Maslow's theory 15 years later.

## *Harry Harlow's Primates and Lessons in Love*

Harry Harlow grew alarmed at the implications of Maslow's theory and its widespread adoption. Experts began telling parents that their children didn't need them. As long as the child received food, water, clothing, and adequate shelter, they would be fine. It didn't matter who provided it.

Harry foresaw the disastrous consequences this would have on young, developing minds. He set out to prove it with a series of cruel experiments on primates. First, infant monkeys were taken from their mothers and put into a case with two "surrogate" mothers. One was a wire frame dummy with milk. The other was given a "face" and a terry cloth towel wrapped around it, but no milk. Infant monkeys inevitably preferred the terry cloth mother to the wire frame dummy mother, clinging to it even to the point of starvation. Food did not provide adequate motivation to leave "her" behind.

Next, he put older primates in a pit and gave them everything they needed except contact with people or other monkeys. Within days, the monkeys refused all food and water. They chose to die rather than live without love. And so do we.

Twenty years after Harry Harlow's primate experiments ended, Bruce Alexander began conducting Rat Park experiments in an effort to find the root causes of addiction and its cure. I'll share what Bruce learned about addiction and its relationship to love next.

## *Bruce Alexander and the Roots of Addiction*

Bruce Alexander conducted his Rat Park experiments from 1978-1981. During the first round of his experiments, he took rats away from their normal, social environment and placed them in cages. They were given all the food they needed along with clean shelter. They provided the rats two water bottles: one that was laced with morphine and the other containing pure water.

Without fail, the rats would drink the drugged water until they overdosed. At first, Bruce blamed this on the addictive power of the drug. Then, he realized something: He'd taken the rats out of their native habitat. What if it was the isolation - not the drugs themselves - killing the rats?

Sure enough, rats placed in their native social habitat either ignored the drugged water altogether or took a few sips of it here and there but didn't develop an addiction or overdose from its use. Their need for love was being met.

Now that you're beginning to get an understanding of what the science says about the importance of love, let's do a few exercises.

## *Exercises:*

Journal your answer to the following questions:

1. Do you believe you are loved?

2. Do you believe you are lovable?

3. If the answer to either question is no, why don't you believe it to be true?

4. If the answer to either question is yes, what evidence proves to you that the statement is true?

5. Is the evidence you're using to prove that someone loves you causing you to miss out on the love they are trying to show you?

## *Let's Pray:*

Lord Jesus Christ, you came that we might experience the fullness of God's love for us. I ask you to reveal to me all those things that are standing in the way of me receiving your love and giving it to others. Help me to let go of the pain of my past so that I can open up to the abundance of love and healing you have for me in each present moment. I ask all this in the power of your Most Holy and Sacred Name. Amen.

## *What's Next?*

Now that you understand the need for love and how important it is to us, let's talk about why human love just isn't ever going to be enough.

# CHAPTER 2. THE LIMITS OF HUMAN LOVE

## *Human Love is Limited*

*"To err is human; to forgive, divine." - Alexander Pope, an Essay on Criticism*

No two human beings are biologically capable of seeing things the exact same way. This is because no two of us share the same genetics, family history, life experience, education, knowledge, skills, talents, and gifts. Miscommunication and misunderstandings are inevitable because of these differences.

These miscommunications and misunderstandings can damage our relationships. That damage interferes with our ability to give and receive love.

Imagine that we are all clay jugs fashioned and shaped for the purpose of catching the love that falls all around us and pouring it out onto others. Now, imagine that every time we get hurt in a relationship, it's like a pebble's been thrown at that jug and a little piece of us falls to the ground.

Enough pieces chip off and a hole opens up in the wall of that jug. Now, we can't hold onto any of the love that we receive. It all pours out of us just as soon as it enters in and we don't have any to give to others.

To restore the flow of love, we need to forgive. But that's easier said than done. Let's talk about the biological challenges we face in forgiving ourselves and others.

## *Our Biology Works Against Us*

Our brains are hard-wired to remember and protect us against anything or anyone that causes us pain. It sees these emotional events as important to our survival to remember, so it bypasses our normal memory process and stamps them right onto the core memories we carry.

This makes the process of letting go and releasing the pain, which is required for us to forgive, difficult. Depending on the level of pain caused by the offending incident, it can be impossible without outside intervention.

Yet if we don't forgive, it blocks our ability to give and receive love. Let's explore the other reasons that human love can fail us.

## *Human Love is Guaranteed to Fail*

Infatuation is like inspiration: It gets things started, but it won't keep them going. Those initial feelings of passion and connection will fade in the face of reality. They're not real love.

Emotions change from moment to moment and day to day. Love based on emotions shifts like sand. Relationships built on emotions collapse eventually because they don't have a solid enough foundation.

Committed love comes after infatuation disappears. When love is a choice you make instead of a feeling, it's got the staying power to last. However, that kind of love requires choosing to make continual acts of self-sacrifice and self-denial. Those acts defy our instincts for self-preservation and survival.

Then, there's death. No human being, no matter how sainted, can avoid death. It comes for us all eventually, and there's no way around that fact. No matter how good or how loving a human being may be, their love will eventually fail us.

The limits of our ability to forgive and to allow ourselves to be forgiven determine the limits of our ability to give and receive love.

Now that we've looked at the reasons why human love is limited and not enough to meet our needs, let's engage in some exercises to help us explore these concepts more.

## *Exercises*

Journal your answers to the following questions:

1. When is a time you can think of that human love failed you?

2. Have you forgiven the person who failed to love you?

3. Why or why not?

4. When is a time that you can think of when your love failed someone else?

5. Have you forgiven yourself for that failure to love?

6. Why or why not?

7. If you've been able to forgive, what steps did you take to achieve a state of forgiveness?

## *Let's Pray:*

Lord Jesus Christ, you forgive me every wrong I commit and you love me in spite of those things. Your love never fails me, and it never gives up on me. Help me to open up my heart to receive your forgiveness and to accept your love. Help me to forgive all those who wrong me and teach me how to love those around me in spite of the things they've done. Help me never to give up on love. I ask all this in the power of your Most Holy and Sacred Name. Amen.

## *What's Next?*

Now that we understand our need for love and why human love isn't going to be enough to satisfy us, let's talk about the role that God plays in fulfilling our need for love.

z

# CHAPTER 3. THE NEED FOR GOD

## *Perfect Love is Impossible for Human Beings...But Not for God*

"...for God is love" – 1 John 4:8

## *What Can We Do When Human Love Isn't Enough?*

We all need love to live, but - as we showed in the last lesson - human love isn't enough. Whether it happens due to biological differences, misunderstandings or miscommunications, selfish instincts, or death, we know that human love will fail.

We can't give one another perfect love because we don't have it to give. It's simple logic: only a being that loves perfectly can give us perfect love. Only that being can provide us with the tools needed to love perfectly. It's beyond our human capacity.

Now that we've established that only a being of perfect love can give us perfect love, let's look at the requirements for us to find infinite, eternal love.

## *Providing Infinite, Eternal Love*

Limited, Finite Beings Can't Provide Infinite, Eternal

Love. Every human being comes with limits that are physical, emotional, mental, and spiritual. We may reach our limits in a hurry, or it may take us time, but we will reach them eventually. Even if we become capable of loving perfectly in our lifetime, our life itself comes with limits.

Again, we can't give one another what we don't have to give. Only God's infinite and eternal love can make our love both infinite and eternal. If we try and rely on human beings to provide this to us, we are going to find ourselves always hungering for what we don't have and can't get.

We'll explore what Jesus Christ stated about where we can find a source of perfect, infinite, eternal love.

## *God: Wellspring of Perfect, Undying Love*

*"Jesus answered her, 'Anyone who drinks such water as this will be thirsty again afterwards, the man who drinks the water I give him will not know thirst any more. The water I give him will be a spring of water within him, that flows continually to bring him everlasting life.'" - John 4:14*

God alone offers the perfect, unconditional, infinite source of undying love that every human being needs in order to make life worth living and eternal life possible. But He won't force it on us. We must choose to receive it from Him and pass it on to others.

*"...for man this is impossible, but with God all things are possible." - Matthew 19:26*

Now that we're clear about why God is a necessity for man's happiness in this life and the next, let's work through the exercises to apply what we've learned.

## *Exercises*

Journal your answers to the following questions:

1. Do you believe that God exists?

2. Why or why not?

3. If you do believe He exists, do you believe that God loves you?

4. What are ways that you know God loves you?

5. Why would that be proof of God's love?

6. Do you ever doubt God's love?

7. If you don't believe God loves you, what causes you to doubt God's love?

8. Why would that be proof God doesn't love you?

## *Let's Pray*

Lord God, I want to receive your perfect, infinite, unconditional, and eternal love. I want to live in the grace of your love and allow it to transform my life. I ask that you open my heart to accept your love, and that you remove everything in my life that is currently blocking the path of that love from reaching me. I ask all this in the power of your Most Holy and Sacred Name, Lord Jesus Christ. Amen.

## *What's Next?*

Now that we understand why God is essential to the human need for love, let's talk about one of the greatest mysteries of the Christian faith: The Holy Trinity and how it all ties back to love.

# CHAPTER 4. THE HOLY TRINITY OF LOVE

*"May the God of hope fill you with all joy and peace in believing, so that by the power of the Holy Spirit you may abound in hope." - Romans 15:13*

One of the most difficult aspects of understanding Christianity is the concept of a triune God. One that is three unique, separate, and distinct persons in one indivisible God.

In mathematical terms, you might say that God is 1 cubed (1 to the power of 3). Just as a triangle can have three sides that are separate and distinct from one another yet all be part of the same triangle, so it is with God the Father, God the Son, and God the Holy Spirit.

Looked at through the lens of God being love, however, it takes on a new light. He is the perfect, indivisible, eternal union of love, hope, and joy. Hope and joy are never found when love isn't present.

## God the Father: Unfailing, Eternal Love

As we learned in the last lesson, God is love but not in a human sense. He is love that is unfailing, unlimited, and eternal.

He is a father in that He creates all things. Love is where all things begin and love is the purpose for which all things are created.

Now that we understand the role that God plays in this trinity of love, hope, and joy, mark this lesson complete and let's explore the Son and His role in the Holy Trinity.

## *God the Son: Love's Eternal, Undying Hope Made Flesh*

As often as mankind rejected God's love and His call to live in love with one another, God never gave up hope that we could be saved. He never quit trying to reach us. He continues doing so even today through you and me.

Jesus Christ is the fullest expression of that undying, eternal hope for humanity. Jesus Christ shows just how far God is willing to go to demonstrate His love for us. His love took Him to the point where He entered into a sacred union with the Blessed Virgin Mary, conceiving a child with her, so that He might become 100% human while retaining 100% of His divinity. Jesus Christ is God's only begotten Son in that He is the only son of God's begotten of a human woman.

When humanity turned against Him, rather than destroy us, He gave up His life to save us. He allowed Himself to be put to death for our sake so that He could conquer death through his resurrection and open up the gates of Heaven, offering us eternal life.

If you're ready to uncover the Holy Spirit's connection to the Holy Trinity and the role He plays in this, let's move forward.

## *God the Holy Spirit: The Unending Joy That Love Brings and the Peace of Undying Hope*

*"And there shall come forth a rod out of the root of Jesse, and a blossom shall come up from his root: and the Spirit of God shall rest upon him, the spirit of wisdom and understand-*

*ing, the spirit of counsel and strength, the spirit of knowledge and Godliness shall fall on him. The spirit of the fear of God."*
*- Isaiah 11:1-2*

The love between God the Father and God the Son bursts forth into an unending joy that is the Holy Spirit. That joy brings with it peace beyond all understanding.

With the Holy Spirit comes seven gifts that enable us to live in love:

1. Knowledge
2. Wisdom
3. Understanding
4. Counsel
5. Fortitude
6. Piety
7. Fear of the Lord

*"These things I have spoken to you, that my joy may be in you, and your joy may be filled." - John 15:11*

Now that we've got a clearer picture of the Trinity and its role in helping humanity live in love and experience the fullness of hope and joy, let's get onto the exercises that will help us grow in our understanding.

## *Exercises*

Journal your answers to the following questions:

1. Do you feel that your life is filled with love, hope, and joy?
2. If not, which of the three is most lacking in your life?
3. What would change in your life if you could be filled with love, hope, and joy at all times?
4. What are you willing to sacrifice to experience that?

## *Let's Pray:*

Holy Spirit, you are the bringer of all good gifts. Grant me the gift of invincible hope, unending joy, and the unfailing love of Jesus Christ. I ask all this in the power of the most Holy and Sacred name of our Lord, Jesus Christ. Amen.

## *What's Next?*

Now that we've hopefully gotten a better grasp on what the Holy Trinity is and how that works, let's dive into another tough topic: Heaven, Hell, and Purgatory. We're going to be discussing how the existence of those three things provides proof that God loves us - and what it means when we say those words.

z

# CHAPTER 5. FINDING LOVE IN HEAVEN, HELL, AND PURGATORY

## *Love Requires Free Will*

*"I have come that they may have life, and that they may have it more abundantly."- John 10:10*

Love cannot be forced. If love can't be rejected, it becomes forced. Forced love is coercion, and never genuine.

I can tie you up and put you in a locked room. I can tell you, "I'm not letting you go until you tell me that you love me." You may say the words, but they would be meaningless. I could never be sure that you meant them. You might be saying them just to buy back your freedom.

Only if I let you go and you are free to choose to be with me or to leave me will I ever know for sure you mean those words. Authentic love requires being able to choose to reject the love that's offered.

That's the purpose of free will: It creates the room for genuine, authentic love to exist. Now that we've established the purpose of free will, let's talk about why Hell is a necessary component of God's love.

## *Hell: Life Without Love*

> *But I say to you that everyone who is angry with his brother will be liable to judgment; whoever insults his brother will be liable to the council; and whoever says, 'You fool!' will be liable to the hell of fire. – Matthew 5:25*

Hell is a space carved out for those who choose to reject God's love. God did not desire for man to be sent there. He created it for the fallen angels who did not wish to live under God's laws and serve humanity.

However, if men choose to reject love, that is where He sends them, honoring their choices. They receive what they chose: an eternity without the presence of God's infinite love, hope, and joy.

> *"I call Heaven and Earth to witness against you today, that I have set before you life and death, the blessing and the curse. So choose life in order that you may live, you and your descendants."- Deuteronomy 30:19*

Ask any person who ever experienced it, and they can confirm this for you: life without love, hope, or joy feels like Hell.

Instead of being filled with love, hope, and joy which bring you peace beyond all understanding, you live a life filled with despair for your future, rage over your impotence to change things, and loathing for all those who have what you can't get. Instead of finding peace, your world is filled with anxiety.

Those who reject love and its call to live a life of selfless sacrifice on behalf of others are choosing to embrace the hell of life without love, hope, or joy. That's because, as we discussed earlier, hope and joy come from love. They are an indivisible unity and an inseparable package. Only when you are filled with love, hope, and joy can you find that perfect peace the world cannot give.

Plenty of people actively choose to reject love out of fear that they aren't worthy of love, aren't good enough to be loved, or are too sinful and too broken for love to be able to reach them. That's not true, but they believe it to be true. That belief blocks them from being able to accept God's efforts to reach them.

Some people reject love because they fear the sacrifices that will be required in order to make room for love's constant presence in their life. They miss out on the fullness of hope and joy that could have been theirs as a result.

God will not force anyone to choose Him, since that would not be love at all. He will allow you to reject love even when that's not His preferred will. That choice to reject love is what causes people to be condemned to Hell. It's not God condemning us. It's us condemning us by rejecting His love.

Hopefully you now have a better understanding of Hell is – and its necessity for us to experience genuine love - let's talk about what Heaven is and what makes it so good.

## *Heaven: Life with Perfect Love, Hope, and Joy*

Heaven is God's kingdom. It's that place where love, hope, and joy reign supreme. God's love forms the rules and those rules are followed by all who live there, not because they have to, but because it brings them unending joy to do so.

We don't have to wait for eternity to begin experiencing Heaven on Earth. We begin experiencing it to the degree that we surrender our lives to love and let love, hope, and joy take ownership of our hearts.

This is the promise of the Our Father:

*"Thy kingdom come, thy will be done on earth as it is in Heaven." - Matthew 6:10*

When God's will for us to prioritize love above all things and to love one another as He loves us is done, His kingdom will come into our hearts and we will experience Heaven right here on Earth.

Now that you have a better understanding of what Hell is and how you get there, as well as what Heaven is, and why both are part of love, let's talk about Purgatory.

## *Purgatory: Redeeming the Past to Restore Love*

Every time we choose to reject love, we open up wounds in our hearts that make it harder for us to choose love. That difficulty in loving others spills out onto the people around us, creating wounds in their hearts. This damage transmits itself from person to person and generation to generation from that point forward.

When we confess our sins and are sincere in our sorrow for them, Jesus heals our hearts. He gives us the courage to set things right with the people we've harmed when we rejected .

We can then face up to the damage we've caused by what we've done and work to repair things. However, if we don't manage to set right all the damage we did by rejecting love while we're alive, we're given the chance to set things right in Purgatory.

In Purgatory, our hearts burn with love for God, but we're in a state of physical separation from Him. While it's true, as stated in Romans 8: 39, that "neither the height above us nor the depth beneath us, nor any other created thing, will be able to separate us from the love of God, which comes to us in Christ Jesus our Lord," we choose not to enter the Kingdom of Heaven just yet because we recognize we need to prepare ourselves first.

Imagine it like this. You've got a terrible drug addiction but you're working to give it up. It caused you to hurt those you love most, and you don't ever want to hurt them that same way again.

You check yourself into a rehab unit because you know that you aren't ready to go home until you've got that addiction fully under control. The separation is incredibly painful, but it's a necessary part of your healing.

What keeps you going is knowing that love, hope, and joy are waiting for you when you're ready to return. But to protect your family from your own shortcomings, you've got to stay away until you can shake the addiction.

Faithful Catholics experience a small taste of this whenever they make a decision to do something they know offends God and then repent of it. We keep ourselves from going to communion and allowing ourselves to be fully united to Christ until we go to confession and ask for God's help in healing the wounds we caused by our failure to love Him above all things – including our own will.

It's tough wanting to be united to Christ, but knowing that doing it before we've received that confession would be like giving Jesus a kiss on the cheek before betraying Him to the guards.

It's also like a woman who commits adultery and repents of it, but doesn't tell her husband about it or make an effort to make amends for it. Sex is meant to be the greatest unifier of a married couple, but the lie between them would make a true union impossible. Only when she's willing to be open with her husband and honest about her failings can he forgive her and the two of them become truly one again. Communion is meant to be the greatest unifier between Christ and His bride, but it can't be that when we're holding back from admitting to what we've done and sincerely repenting of it.

The pain of that separation would be unbearable if not for the hope and joy that we experience because of our love for Him. As it is, we are unable to do anything for ourselves.

Everything we do in Purgatory is done for others, without acknowledgment or thanks. We offer our suffering and our prayers for the souls who might otherwise be lost because of the damage our failures caused while living on Earth.

We must rely on the prayers of those who remember us on Earth for our release from Purgatory. When someone prays for our release, it becomes a sign we've helped to heal the damage we caused by rejecting God's love in our earthly life.

## *Once We Enter Eternity, Our Final Decision Is Made*

*"Teach us to count every passing day, till our hearts find wisdom." - Psalm 90:12*

God made time so that mankind might appreciate life and ultimately choose the best way to use it. While we live, He grants us the ability to choose what we will do. We can always change our minds at any time.

We can choose to leave behind a path of selfishness and choose instead to selflessly follow Christ. Our habits may make leaving behind our old ways harder, but if we truly desire to live for Christ, we can.

God gives us every reason and opportunity possible to choose love rather than rejecting it, but He can't force us to choose love or it wouldn't be love at all.

Once we enter eternity, time ceases to exist. We are frozen in whatever state we chose in our last moment. Change is no longer possible.

## *Exercises*

Journal your answers to the following questions:

1. Which does your life currently resemble more: Heaven, Hell, or Purgatory?

2. Which would you like it to resemble more?

3. Do you want to live an eternity like you are right now?

4. Are you ready to choose to live a life solely for the sake of love?

5. Why or why not?

## *Let's Pray:*

Lord Jesus Christ, you came that I might know the truth about love. You encourage me to dedicate my life to love. I reject a life without love and I ask that you uproot everything in my life that is causing me to turn away from love. Dissolve those roots in the blood of your mercy and cleanse my heart with the water that flowed from your side. I ask you to redeem my past, restore my present, and secure my future that I might walk with you in the way of love all the days of my life. I ask all this in the power of your Most Holy and Sacred Name. Amen.

## *What's Next?*

Now that we've talked about why God is necessary for human beings to get their need for love perfectly met, and the dangers of choosing to reject love, let's talk about organized religion and its role in helping us to live lives of love.

z

# CHAPTER 6. HUMANITY'S NEED FOR ORGANIZED RELIGION

Having proven the need for God's love, let's tackle the next big obstacle: the need for organized religion. I've encountered many a person who tells me, "I'm spiritual, but not religious" or who blames organized religion for every problem in mankind. I've also encountered those who will, wrongly, tell you that God or Jesus didn't establish a religion.

## *Defining Religion*

The Oxford Dictionary defines religion as the belief in and worship of a superhuman power, especially a god or gods. It can also refer to the activities associated with the worship of a god or gods.

However, that definition fails humanity. It looks only at what is being done, rather than why these things are being done. What is the function the rules serve?

Because, if we're to assume that these rules and laws are passed down by a god or gods, we need to start with the assumption that there's a purpose to the rules. They shouldn't be either random or meaningless.

Religion, in its simplest terms, is a set of rules about relationships. It defines what is okay to do to yourself or others and what is not okay. If you don't belong to an organized religion, you're going to be making up your own rules as you go along.

That's leaving you in the unenviable position of needing to reinvent the wheel in terms of figuring out which rules are helpful and which are harmful. That leads to disorganized chaos!

## *Relationships Are Required for Love to Flourish*

Man needs love to give life meaning and purpose, but love can't exist apart from relationships. Religion plays a defining role in meeting humanity's need for love by providing structured, time-tested, and psychologically proven-to-work rules for forming healthy, loving relationships that are life-giving and meaningful.

All of religion's rules center on relationships:

1. With our Creator and source of love
2. With ourselves
3. With our families
4. With society
5. With those who believe as we do
6. With those who don't
7. With other species
8. With our environment

Now that we know what role religion serves in helping us to experience the fullest expression of love possible, let's talk about what happens when we subtract love from our religious practices.

## *Religion Without Love*

Not all religions believe that humanity was created for love, by love, and for the purpose of being loved. When we subtract love from the equation of religion, it becomes a set of:

**R**igid

*E*xpectations
*L*egalistic
*I*ndoctrinations
*G*rowing
*I*nconsistencies
*O*verbearing
*N*osiness

Nobody wants that. It leaves us feeling locked up, confined, and unable to move forward. That's the kind of religion that gets people running in the opposite direction, desperate to find a way out the doors.

When religion looks like this, it's a sure sign that human egos are at work, NOT God's love. The human ego thrives on feeling superior to other people, but that's toxic to our ability to enter into loving relationships. Given a chance, we end up turning laws that are meant to benefit and help us into nooses that hang and suffocate us. We end up divided rather than united.

## *Religion with Love*

Contrary to popular belief, God did create a religion. He created a set of definitive rules for relationships. Those rules are designed to help us live out His call for us to love one another.

When religion is lived with love it looks like this:

*R*espectful
*E*mpathy
*L*oving
*I*ntentions
*G*uided
*I*nstruction
*O*ngoing
*N*urturing

I've yet to meet anyone who doesn't want that. The reality is that rules provide boundaries that help us to know what's safe to do and what's not. We don't have to reinvent the relationship wheel every generation, trying to figure out what works and what doesn't.

If we follow the right religion, we learn how to avoid doing the things that hurt other people and damage our relationships. We also learn how to deepen our relationships and get access to the things we need to grow in our capacity for giving and receiving love. Let's explore this concept more in the exercises.

**Remember: Rules alone are not enough to help humanity live out the call to love.**

## *Exercises*

Journal your answers to the following questions:

1. Which version of religion are you used to seeing?
2. How does your past experience with religion color your expectations for religion?
3. Would you like to experience the second version of religion?
4. If not, why not?
5. If so, are you prepared to offer that second version of religion to others?
6. If not, why not?

## *Let's Pray:*

Lord God, you established all order that is in the universe. All things operate by rules that you created, and it is only when we surrender to those rules that we can live in harmony with one another and with the universe. Where my life is out of order, I ask that you come and help me to accept your rules and to embrace the order that you created. Where I am in rebellion against your rules, I ask that you help me to understand these rules and how they connect to love so that I might operate in the grace of obedience to your will and your plan for love. I ask all this in the power of the Most Holy and Sacred Name of Jesus Christ. Amen.

## *What's Next?*

Now that we've established what organized religion does to help man live out his call to love so he can overcome the challnges, it's time to walk through how we can discern which religion is the right religion to follow. After all, there are more than 50,000 different denominations of Christianity alone and thousands of other religions on top of it. It can be a daunting through to try and sort through them all.

z

# CHAPTER 7. CHOOSING THE RIGHT RELIGION

If love is the most primal need every human being has - and we've demonstrated that it is - then the right religion is the religion that helps us fill our lives with love to the fullest capacity.

Not all religions are alike. Not all religions provide everything that human beings need to be able to live love to the fullest.

No matter how good a religion may be, if it does not provide a perfect model of love to follow, it is inadequate to the task of helping humanity live love to our fullest capacity.

We need:

1. The right rules to provide us with guidance in choosing love in all circumstances

2. The right models of perfect love in operation to learn from and emulate

3. The right support systems to help us choose love at all times

4. A community to practice our skills in giving and receiving love

5. Clear and unambiguous leadership pointing the way

to love

Without those five things, we flounder and get lost on the road to love. Mark this lesson complete, and let's discuss what perfect love looks like and where we can find it.

## *Perfect Love Requires a Perfect Model*

All human beings learn the most from seeing behavior modeled for them. That's why healthy, loving families are so important to a healthy, loving society: these families model for their children what healthy love looks like and help them to live it.

No other religion, apart from Christianity, provides a perfect model of human love lived to its fullest capacity. We get a male role model in Christ, and a female role model in His mother, Mary. That ensures both genders can see how love in action is meant to be lived.

Christ provides the perfect model of love lived out in the face of the absolute worst that humanity could throw at Him. Ridiculed, scorned, abused, betrayed, abandoned, mocked, falsely accused, condemned despite His innocence, He choose to allow humanity to put Him to death in one of the worst ways imaginable: a crucifixion.

Suffocating and dying an agonizing death on the cross, He still chose to forgive us all, telling God,

> *"Father, forgive them, for they know not what they do."* - Luke 23:34

Mary provides the perfect model of a life lived for Christ. From the very moment of her Annunciation, when the Angel Gabriel appeared to her to let her know she'd been chosen to give birth to Christ, she dedicated her life to serving her son. Every plan she'd made before that point she abandoned.

She stood by Him during every moment of His suffering on the cross. She didn't interfere with His mission or beg Him to come down from the cross. She supported Him in the only way she could, by being present with Him. When He told her, as one of His last acts,

> *"Woman, behold your son."* - *John 19:26*

she didn't hesitate to accept her new assignment.

She took on all who were Jesus's beloved disciples as her own - even those who betrayed, abused, and abandoned Him during His moment of greatest need. She loved them until her last breath on Earth and continues to love them in eternity.

Now that we understand what makes these two perfect role models for living a life of love, let's mark this lesson complete and examine what sets the Catholic Church apart from all other Christian denominations when it comes to living our call to love.

## *What Catholicism Alone Provides*

When it comes to living a life of love, no Christian denomination is superior to what the Catholic Church provides those who enter into her union with Christ.

They receive the total package, all five things needed, to help them live lives of love:

1. Every rule, teaching, and practice is geared toward helping her members live out our call to love.

2. Perfect role models in Jesus and Mary and relatable role models in the Saints

3. A Supernatural Support system in the 7 Sacraments and the priesthood

4. A community for practicing the skills required to grow in love

5. Clear, unambiguous leadership pointing the way toward love through the doctrine of papal infallibility and the Magisterium

While the Catholic Church is often accused of being nothing more than a set of man-made rules, it's survived for over 2,000 years because it taps into the spiritual rules, laws, principles, and practices provided by Jesus Christ.

In addition, it offers every supernatural help necessary for human beings to maximize their capacity to give and receive love. If you want to live a meaningful life filled with the peace that comes from love, hope, and joy, you need look no further.

Now that you know what the Catholic Church provides that other religions and other Christian denominations don't, let's work through the exercises.

## *Exercises*

Journal your answer to the following questions:

1. What is your past experience with the Catholic Church?
2. What is your past experience with Christianity?
3. Does this lesson inspire you to re-examine your thoughts about what Christianity – and the Catholic faith – offer you?
4. In what ways?
5. How will you apply this new understanding to your life going forward?

## *Let's Pray*

Lord Jesus Christ, you offer us a perfect model of love in your life and in your death. You provide us a perfect model of what it means to follow you in your mother, Mary. You give us the Church and the undivided unity she promotes. Help me to receive these gifts from you with an open heart and an open mind. Help me to see more clearly where I am rejecting your gifts and to remove from my life the things that are stopping me from accepting the graces that these gifts offer me in living a life of love. I ask all this in the power of your Most Holy and Sacred Name. Amen.

## *What's Next?*

We've touched a bit on Jesus and His role in providing humanity hope. Let's talk about what makes Him the perfect model of love.

# CHAPTER 8. JESUS, THE PERFECT MODEL OF LOVE

## *Jesus Christ: God's Perfect Love and Eternal Hope for Humanity Made Flesh*

> *"For God so loved the world, that He gave His only begotten Son, that whosoever believeth in Him should not perish, but have everlasting life." - John 3:16*

Despite all of our choices to reject God from the very beginning, God never lost hope in Humanity. It is this hope that is the reason He sent Jesus Christ to become one with us during the Incarnation. In His death, He shows us how much He loves us even when we are at our worst.

Jesus Christ is God's Perfect love and Eternal hope for Humanity in human flesh. Now that we know the role that Christ plays in helping us to better understand God's love, let's discuss what is meant when we say that Jesus is the Way, the Truth, and the Life.

## *Jesus: The Way, the Truth, and the Life*

> *"Jesus saith to him: I am the way, and the truth, and the life. No man cometh to the Father, but by me." - John 14:6*

In Jesus's life, He showed us the Way God expected us to love one another by His actions and His teachings.

In Jesus's death, He demonstrated the Truth about what it takes to love. He showed us that love is a choice made to sacrifice your own life for the good of others, even when those others don't appreciate the sacrifice you're making.

*"Greater love than this no man hath, that a man lay down his life for his friends." - John 15:13*

He lived His entire Life dedicated to love. Following His teachings and example is how we learn to live out Christ's call to

*"Love one another as I have loved you." - John 13:34*

## The Crucifixion's Necessity

Only for Christ could the crucifixion be a freely willed choice made to sacrifice His life in order to save Humanity. Only for Christ could the crucifixion be a true act of love.

Without that sacrifice, humanity doesn't get a perfect example of love for all people - even those who betray, abuse, abandon, steal from, falsely accuse and condemn, ridicule, scorn, reject, or who are passive in the face of injustices committed against us.

In Jesus, all of these things took place. And still He chose to love us and to desire our greatest possible good - an eternity spent filled with love, hope, and joy - and to do what was necessary to see to it the opportunity to receive that gift was not denied us.

He forgave them all and, because He died in that state of forgiveness, His forgiveness is eternal. No matter what we do or have done, He will forgive it if we allow Him to do so. He will forgive us as often as we come to Him, repenting of our sin and desiring to set things right.

*"...the message of the cross is foolishness to those who are perishing, but to us who are being saved it is the power of God." - 1 Corinthians 1:18*

Now that we see why the Crucifixion was necessary for love to flourish and thrive, let's engage in some exercises.

## *Exercises*

Journal your answers to the following questions:

1. Does this answer your questions about the necessity of the Crucifixion?

2. If not, what questions remain for you?

3. Offer those questions up to Christ and ask Him to answer them for you.

4. How does it feel to know that Christ is proof of God's unfailing hope in humanity?

5. Does this help you better understand what is meant by Jesus being the Way, the Truth, and the Life?

6. If not, where do you remain confused?

7. Ask God to help you understand the things that don't make sense to you.

8. If so, how will you apply that understanding to your life?

## *Let's Pray:*

Lord Jesus Christ, you are the Way, the Truth, and the Life. May I follow your way, walk in your truth, and live a life dedicated to love, just as you did. Help me to grow in my understanding of and appreciation for your sacrifice on the Cross that I might share this understanding and appreciation with all that I encounter. I ask all this in the power of your most Holy and Sacred Name. Amen.

## *What's Next?*

Now that we can see how Jesus is the perfect model of love, let's talk more about what He did, through His words and in His crucifixion, to answer humanity's greatest questions about love.

z

# CHAPTER 9. JESUS: ANSWERING HUMANITY'S GREATEST QUESTIONS ABOUT LOVE

### *Showing Us How to Love the Unlovable*

*"But I say to you who hear: Love your enemies, do good to those who hate you..." - Luke 6:27*

From the beginning, God commanded those who called themselves His people to:

*"Do not seek revenge or bear a grudge against anyone among your people, but love your neighbor as yourself." - Leviticus 19:18*

But that left humanity with questions:

1. Who counts as my neighbor?

2. How far must I go in loving them?

3. Where are the limits in forgiving others?

Now that we know what their questions were, let's see what answers Christ provided.

### *Christ's Answer to: "Who Counts as My Neighbor?"*

On the day of the Crucifixion, members of all known nations were present in Jerusalem. As a result, representatives from all races and peoples participated - either directly or indirectly - in His crucifixion.

They either participated in it directly by contributing to it or helping others to contribute to it, or they participated passively by not raising up an objection and trying to stop it.

Thus, Christ's answer to the question of who counts as my neighbor: Everyone.

Even that neighbor who abuses, mistreats, betrays, slanders, denies that they know you when you need their help the most, or is indifferent to you and your suffering.

## *Christ's Answer to: "How Far Must I Go in Loving My Neighbor as Myself?"*

Christ's willingness to die to redeem us from our sins answers the question of how far we must go to love our neighbor as ourselves: all the way to our last breath.

Simply put: Love sets no limits.

We are to continue loving our neighbor even to the point of death regardless of whether they choose to accept that love or reject it. There is no other way.

This does not mean that we must participate with them in everything they do or agree with them in everything they say. Rather, we must continue praying for them and striving to help them find Christ no matter how much they hurt us or how often they reject our efforts.

## *Christ's Answer to: "What Are the Limits to Forgiveness?"*

> *Your heavenly Father will forgive you your transgressions, if you forgive your fellow men theirs; if you do not forgive them, your heavenly Father will not forgive your transgressions either. - Matthew 6:14-15*

Christ forgave every sin humankind ever committed or will commit on that cross without hesitation.

His answer: Forgiveness must know no limits.

A refusal to forgive is a refusal to love. Love's limits begin where forgiveness ends.

God forgives every sin - but to benefit from that gift, one must choose to accept it. The people in Hell chose to refuse that gift, either by refusing to allow themselves to be forgiven or by refusing to forgive others.

Now that we know what Christ's answers were to humanity's three greatest questions about love, let's get started on the exercises.

## *Exercises*

Journal your answers to the following questions:

1. How do I feel about the call to forgive without limits?

2. How do I feel about the call to see everyone as my neighbor?

3. Am I prepared to love all those who hate me and bless all those who persecute me?

4. If not, am I willing to ask God to help me to be prepared to do those things?

5. Am I ready to accept that if I reject the call to forgive, I am rejecting love and choosing Hell instead?

6. Do I believe the people whose failures to love me hur me so much are worth giving up my place in Heaven just to hold onto the pain they caused me?

7. If so, why are they worth living an eternity of agony over?

## *Let's Pray*

Holy Spirit, you are the Spirit of love and the Spirit of Forgiveness. Inspire my heart to love and to forgive all those who have hurt me in the past, all those who hurt me in the present, and all those who will hurt me in the future. Fill me with your grace and your presence so that I can love as Christ loves me. I ask all this in the power of the Most Holy and Sacred Name of Jesus Christ. Amen.

## *What's Next?*

We've explored the necessity of the crucifixion and the answers Christ's life provided to humanity's questions about love. Now, let's talk about the necessity of the resurrection and what it says about love.

# CHAPTER 10. THE NECESSITY OF THE RESURRECTION

## *Conquering Death*

> *"Jesus told her, 'I am the resurrection and the life. Anyone who believes in me will live, even after dying. Everyone who lives in me and believes in me will never ever die.'"* - John 11:25-26

If Jesus did not die, He could not conquer death. In conquering death, He conquered our fear of dying. He set us free to love without fear and to give unselfishly to others even in our own need.

Now that we know why His resurrection matters, let's explore what else His resurrection does to help us love.

## *Turning Tragedy into Triumph*

If Christ merely died for us, and did not rise again, His death is merely a tragedy. There's no triumph in it.

It's just another story about a great but poor man crushed beneath the wheels of an elite global superpower. Selfishness and greed triumph over love.

His Resurrection reverses the tragedy, turning it into a triumph over the worst that humanity could do. It demonstrates that love is more powerful than any kind of evil that human beings can do.

Now that we've examined how Jesus's resurrection turns tragedy into a triumph of epic proportions, mark this lesson complete. Let's talk about one of the most important things the resurrection does for us.

## *Restoring Our Hope of Eternal Life*

*"Believe me when I tell you this; the man who has faith in me enjoys eternal life." - John 6:46*

The fall of Adam and Eve removed the access to the Tree of Life for all of humanity. With it went our hope for Eternal Life.

Christ's resurrection restored that hope for us. By following Christ and giving our lives to Him, we can live in eternity with Him.

*"This is a trustworthy saying: If we died with Him, we will also live with Him;" - 2 Timothy 2:11*

Now that we understand why Christ's resurrection matters in terms of helping us live in love, let's engage in our exercises.

## *Exercises*

Journal your answers to the following questions:

1. Do I fear death?

2. If so, how does this fear of death cause me to act in ways that are selfish?

3. If I say that I don't fear death, am I living in a way that reflects my confidence in eternal life?

4. If not, what would I do instead if I put my hopes in Christ's promise of eternal life?

## *Let's Pray*

Lord Jesus Christ, you rose from the dead so that you might render death powerless over men. Help me to trust in your resurrection and to believe in your power. Grant me the graces I need to live my belief in the unfailing power of your love for me. Help me to choose love rather than reject it when I am most tempted to be selfish rather than selfless. I ask all this in the power of your most Holy and Sacred Name. Amen.

## *What's Next?*

Now that we've talked about the necessity of the crucifixion and the resurrection, let's talk about what Christ left us to guide us after the Ascension.

# CHAPTER 11. CHRIST'S PARTING GIFTS: THE HOLY SPIRIT AND THE CATHOLIC CHURCH

## *Keeping Us Moving in Love's Direction*

40 days after Jesus's Resurrection, He ascended into Heaven.

*"When he had said this, they saw him lifted up, and a cloud caught him away from their sight. And as they strained their eyes towards heaven, to watch his journey, all at once two men in white garments were standing at their side. Men of Galilee, they said, why do you stand here looking heavenwards? He who has been taken from you into heaven, this same Jesus, will come back in the same fashion, just as you have watched him going into heaven." - Acts 1:9-11*

But He knew we still needed guidance and support in our journey to loving one another. He knew that, for human beings, loving and forgiving are not easy to do.

*"For man this is impossible, but with God all things are possible." - Matthew 19:26*

He knew that we face numerous biological and psychological obstacles to loving one another. That's why He left behind two primary support mechanisms:

1. The Holy Spirit
2. The Holy Catholic Church.

Let's talk about how those two things help us live lives of authentic love.

## *The Holy Spirit: Equipping Us with an Internal GPS Leading to Love's Timeless Truths*

*"But when the Helper comes, whom I shall send to you from the Father, the Spirit of truth who proceeds from the Father, He will testify of Me." - John 15:26*

The Holy Spirit ensures that every person who follows Christ is equipped with an internal GPS that leads us to love's timeless truths...if we listen.

*"It will be for him, the truth-giving Spirit, when he comes, to guide you into all truth. He will not utter a message of his own; he will utter the message that has been given to him; and he will make plain to you what is still to come." - John 16:13*

Now that you know the role that the Holy Spirit plays in helping us live in love, mark this lesson complete. We'll talk about the gifts that the Holy Spirit brings to those who are open to it.

It is the Holy Spirit, guiding and directing our lives, that also guides and directs the Catholic Church in fulfilling her mission to:

*"Go into all the world and preach the gospel to all creation." - Mark 16:15*

Now that we know what the Holy Spirit does to help us keep moving in the direction of love, let's discuss the Catholic Church's 3-Fold Mission and what that does to help us live lives of authentic love.

## *The Catholic Church's 3-Fold Mission of Love*

*"And I tell you that you are Peter, and on this rock I will build my church, and the gates of Hades will not overcome it." - Matthew 16:18*

The Catholic Church serves Christ in a 3-Fold Mission:

1. To be a visible sign of Christ's presence in the world

2. To preserve and protect the truth about love

3. To ensure God's love remains available to every generation

*"But if I should be delayed, you should know how to behave in the household of God, which is the church of the living God, the pillar and foundation of truth." - 1 Timothy 3:15*

Now that we know the role the Catholic Church plays in keeping people moving in the direction of love, let's engage in some exercises.

## *Exercises*

Journal your answers to the following questions:

1) Do I understand what the Holy Spirit does to help me live a life of authentic love?

2) If not, write down what you don't yet understand. Pray that God would help you to understand it.

3) Do I understand what the Catholic Church's role is in helping me live a life of authentic love?

4) If not, write down what you don't yet understand. Pray that God would help you to understand it.

5) Do I seek the Holy Spirit's guidance when I have questions about the Catholic Church's teachings?

6) If not, am I ready to begin?

7) Do I believe that Christ will never abandon or forsake the Catholic Church?

8) If not, have I prayed over my doubts and asked God for reassurance?

## *Let's Pray:*

God the Father, you sent Jesus Christ into the world to establish a universal Church that would stand for all people and all times. You sent the Holy Spirit into the world to keep us moving in the direction of . You established the Catholic

Church to be that universal sign of your love that would be present and accessible to all throughout the ages so that no weapon formed against your people would prevail. I ask that you help me to bring my doubts, my concerns, my fears, and my hesitations about the Holy Spirit and the Catholic Church to you. I ask that you convict me of the truth so that I may rest in confidence that I am doing your will and living for you alone. I ask all this in the power of the name of your son, Jesus Christ. Amen.

## *What's Next?*

Now that we see what Christ left us, including the Church, to help guide us in the direction of love, let's talk more about the Church's role in preserving and protecting the truth about love.

z

# CHAPTER 12. THE CATHOLIC CHURCH: PRESERVING AND PROTECTING THE TRUTH ABOUT LOVE

## *Ensuring God's Love Remains Available to Every Generation*

The Catholic Church, guided by the Holy Spirit, provides a supernatural support system offering every help necessary for believers to live out the call to love.

*"You who are husbands must shew love to your wives, as Christ shewed love to the Church when he gave himself up on its behalf. He would hallow it, purify it by bathing it in the water to which his word gave life; he would summon it into his own presence, the Church in all its beauty, no stain, no wrinkle, no such disfigurement; it was to be holy, it was to be spotless." - Ephesians 5:25-27*

It is the Church's faithful service to Christ's people that ensures that access to the full teachings of Christ and the apostles remains available to every generation. The Church is not pure, holy, and spotless because the people within her are pure, holy, and spotless.

She is pure, holy, and spotless because she, in perfect obedience to Christ's will, tends to all those whom Christ gathers to Him without prejudice or favor. The Church is a hospital for sinners - and we all have the disease - not a shrine for saints. No one is immune to sin or selfishness.

Now that we've explored a bit more about the Church's role in preserving our access to the Truth about love, let's examine how the Church does this.

## *Safeguarding the Traditions, Holy Scripture, and the 7 Sacraments*

*"Therefore, brethren, stand fast and hold the traditions which you were taught, whether by word or our epistle." - 2 Thessalonians 2:15*

The three things the Catholic Church holds the duty of safeguarding:

1. The Sacred Traditions
2. Holy Scripture
3. The 7 Sacraments

Holy Scripture equips us to know God's love. Sacred Tradition helps us to understand how we are expected to live out that love. And the 7 Sacraments provide the Supernatural Support needed to do so. All of this is to be shared with the community of believers.

Now that we know what role these three things play in helping ensure access to the Truth about love is protected and preserved across all generations, let's look at the final - and irreplaceable - thing the Church provides.

## *Providing a Community in Which to Practice the Skills Needed to Love*

*"Let us not neglect meeting together, as some have made a habit, but let us encourage one another, and all the more as you see the Day approaching." - Hebrews 10:25*

We can love God and be loved by God anywhere we are. However, we cannot obey God's commandments anywhere. God established a Church and He commanded that we gather together as a community of believers at least once a week.

This imperfect gathering of people who are all striving to learn how to live out the call to "love one another as Christ loves us" provides the perfect place for us to practice loving our neighbor. Yes, that neighbor.

The skills required to connect to others, as well as to create, cultivate, and grow relationships are not easy to master and are best done in an environment where people are prepared to forgive one another as mistakes are made. That's what the Church provides.

*"For the husband is the head of the wife as Christ is the head of the Church, his body, of which he is the Savior." - Ephesians 5:23*

It is this body of believers, gathered together as one, that provides an undying, visible sign of Christ's presence in the world. As long as there are two or three gathered in His name, He is there.

*Where two or three are gathered together in my name, I am there in the midst of them. - Matthew 18:20*

Now that we've explored the things the Catholic Church provides to help us live out the call to love, let's get started on the exercises.

## *Exercises*

Journal your answers to the following questions:

1. Do I understand the purpose of the Traditions?

2. If not, write down the things that you don't understand about them.

3. Ask God to show you how He sees it.

4. Do I recognize the value of Holy Scripture?

5. If not, write down your current thoughts about Holy Scripture.

6. Ask God to help you understand its importance.

7. Do I understand the help that the 7 Sacraments provide in living out our call to love?

8. If not, write down what you don't understand about it.

9. Ask God to show you how He sees it.

10. Do I participate in the life of the Church by being involved in the community of believers?

11. If not, why not?

## *Let's Pray*

Holy Spirit, I need your guidance so that I can live in love and follow the example of Christ. Help me to see what I need to see in order to get where I need to be. Open my ears that I might hear the sound of your voice, my eyes that I might see the world as you do, my heart that I might love the world as you do, and my mind that I might think the way you do. I ask all this in the Most Holy and Sacred Power of Jesus Christ. Amen.

## *What's Next?*

We've touched on what the Church does to preserve and protect our access to God's love in every generation. In the next chapter, we're going to dive into more detail on Sacred Tradition.

z

# CHAPTER 13. SACRED TRADITION: WHAT THE APOSTLES HANDED ON ABOUT LOVE

*"Jesus did many other things as well. If every one of them were written down, I suppose that even the whole world would not have room for the books that would be written." - John 21:25*

## *Preserving the "How" Behind "What" Scripture Teaches About Love*

Scripture alone is good, but it isn't enough to help us live out the call to love. It tells us what to do - but not how it is meant to be done.

While the Holy Spirit does help guide us into the how, we are impacted by our biases in how we interpret that guidance. This is why we are not called to rely on our own counsel, but to hold fast to the traditions handed down by the apostles:

*"Stand firm, then, brethren, and hold by the traditions you have learned, in word or in writing, from us." – 2 Thessalonians 2:14*

Scripture is beautiful, but easily misinterpreted. As St. Peter writes:

*"Though indeed, there are passages in them difficult to understand, and these, like the rest of scripture, are twisted into a wrong sense by ignorant and restless minds, to their*

*own undoing." – 2 Peter 3:16*

That's the role that Sacred Tradition plays. It guides us in how we are meant to do all the things that Scripture prescribes for us to do. It provides necessary context for what is being said in Scripture, too. Scripture and Tradition are not rivals to be pitted against one another. They go hand-in-hand.

## *Sacred Tradition Came Before Scripture*

Sacred Tradition is the body of teachings passed down through the ages, first in the Jewish faith and then from Jesus and the apostles, about how we are to live in the light of Scripture. It provides the context and background to the words we find written down.

Sacred Tradition existed long before the first words of the Old Testament were written down. In fact, much of the Old Testament originally existed only in oral form. Those traditions determined which books belonged in Sacred Scripture, and which did not.

The same thing held true in the earliest days of the Church. The Sacred Traditions existed long before the text came along to support them.

To discard Sacred Tradition discards the authority by which Sacred Scripture was established. It removes the very underpinning of Scripture's authority. After all, if those Traditions which decided which books belonged in Scripture and which did not are not valid, neither is the list that it created.

Now that we're clear about Sacred Tradition's role in shaping Sacred Scripture, let's talk about what Sacred Tradition does to help us decode Sacred Scripture.

## *Sacred Tradition Decodes Scripture*

Sacred Tradition provides the key to understanding Scripture. It guides us in understanding the intentions behind it so we can live out those teachings in an authentic way and get the full benefits.

It also helps us live out those teachings in a way that builds love rather than destroys it.

> *"Though indeed, there are passages in them difficult to understand, and these, like the rest of Scripture, are twisted into a wrong sense by ignorant and restless minds, to their own undoing." - 2 Peter 3:16*

Sacred Tradition prevents us from misinterpreting what's being said in Sacred Scripture or how it's meant to be lived out so we don't lose our way and end up following a path to destruction.

## *Safeguarding Sacred Tradition: The Pope and the Magisterium*

Ensuring that the Sacred Traditions of the Catholic Church remain intact from generation to generation is the job of the Magisterium (the teaching body of the Church) and the Pope.

The Magisterium is made up of a union between the Pope, the Cardinals, and the Bishops.

The Pope is the head of the Catholic Church and – with guidance from the Holy Spirit – has the final say. This is because of the authority granted Peter, and all of his successors, by Christ:

> *"I will give you the keys of the kingdom of heaven, and whatever you bind on earth shall be bound in heaven, and whatever you loose on earth shall be loosed in heaven." – Matthew 16:19*

This authority was specific to Peter, which means rock, alone. It was given as a mechanism for fulfilling Christ's promise that:

> *"And I tell you that you are Peter, and on this rock I will build my church, and the gates of Hell will not overcome it." – Matthew 16:18*

The Cardinals serve as papal envoys or diplomats, representing the Church in an official capacity. They are bishops of major diocese, and chief officials of the Roman Curia (the papal bureaucracy).

Bishops are the modern-day apostles. Each is the leader of a single diocese.

> *"Now I praise you because you remember me in everything and hold firmly to the traditions, just as I delivered them to you." - 1 Cor. 11:2*

The Magisterium and the Pope also work together to determine how Scripture applies to modern challenges confronting the Church. Now that you understand the purpose of Sacred Tradition, let's dive into the exercises.

## *Exercises*

Journal your answers to the following questions:

1. What did you know about Sacred Tradition before this lesson?

2. What do you know about it now?

3. What did you believe about it before this lesson?

4. What do you believe about it now?

5. How will this impact your behavior moving forward?

## *Let's Pray:*

Holy Spirit, you guide the development of Sacred Tradition to ensure that Christ's intentions are carried forward into each generation. Please help me to embrace the Sacred Traditions of the Catholic Church and to apply them in the way that I live out my call to love my neighbor as myself. Fill me with trust in your promises and your guidance so that I may operate in obedience to all that Christ willed for me. I ask this in the power of the Most Holy and Sacred Name of Jesus Christ. Amen

## *What's Next?*

Now that we have a better grasp of what role Sacred Tradition plays in preserving the teachings of the apostles and protecting the right of every generation to access the full truth about love, let's talk about what Sacred Scripture does to help us live lives of authentic love.

z

# CHAPTER 14. SACRED SCRIPTURE: THE STORY OF GOD'S LOVE FOR HUMANITY

## *Scripture: A Three-Act Love Story with an Epic Impact*

*"All Scripture is breathed out by God and profitable for teaching, for reproof, for correction, and for training in righteousness, that the man of God may be complete, equipped for every good work." - 2 Timothy 3:16-17*

Despite over 5,000 years between the writing of the first book and the writing of the last, composed by more than 60 different authors across 60 different time periods and cultures, Scripture's most remarkable feature remains how coherent and consistent it is in the story that it tells.

That story ends with an invitation, issued to every generation, to join the battle for love. It also offers a sneak peek at how things turn out for those who need encouragement to make a wise decision.

Having said this, let's explore what the first act of that story holds.

## *Act I: The Old Testament: God's Attempts to Save Humanity from Itself Through Law & Testimony*

The Old Testament is the story of God's unfailing efforts

to save humanity from their repeated decisions to choose the death of selfishness over life with love.

He begins by sending the law to provide clear instructions on how to live out love. He then follows that effort up, when it was clear it wasn't enough, with sending the prophets to communicate His intentions behind the law.

But humanity doesn't get it. They break the law. They kill the prophets. The Chosen people, meant to carry the message of love to humanity, fail to do their duty. They are scattered from the land God gave them and things look bleak.

Let's explore what the second act contains.

## *Act II: The Gospels: God Demonstrates Love By Entering Into the Human Experience*

God, not content to stand by and let humanity kill itself, enters into the human experience. He unites Himself to a virgin named Mary, allowing her to give birth to a child that is both 100% divine and 100% human.

*"When the sixth month came, God sent the angel Gabriel to a city of Galilee called Nazareth, where a virgin dwelt, betrothed to a man of David's lineage; his name was Joseph, and the virgin's name was Mary." - Luke 1: 25-27*

*"And the angel answered her, The Holy Spirit will come upon thee, and the power of the Most High will overshadow thee. Thus this holy offspring of thine shall be known for the Son of God." - Luke 1:35*

This child, Jesus Christ, grows up to model perfect love for us. Now that we know how Act II of this story begins, let's see what Act III holds for us.

## *Act III: Testifying to the Power of Love and Inviting Us to Join the Battle*

The New Testament is where the Third Act begins. It offers us:

•Explorations of the transformation that comes when love

rules your life
• Guidance and encouragement for living lives of authentic love
• Warnings about how to avoid love's counterfeits and the dangers of buying into them
• An invitation to join the battle for love and promises of what to expect when we do

We see what transpires after Christ returns to Heaven and the early Church begins to spread His message with the help of the Holy Spirit. We also get a sneak peek of how the story ends and what is required of those who wish to join the winning side.

*"Whoever believes in me, as the Scripture has said, 'Out of his heart will flow rivers of living water.'" - John 7:38*

Now that we've discussed the three acts present in Scripture, let's engage in the exercises to help us grow in understanding.

## *Exercises*

Journal your answers to the following questions:

1. How did you see the Old Testament before this lesson?

2. How do you see it now?

3. How did you see the Gospels before this lesson?

4. How do you see it now?

5. How did you see the New Testament before this lesson?

6. How do you see it now?

7. How do you feel about Christ's invitation to join the battle for love?

8. Will you choose to accept that invitation or reject it?

9. Why or why not?

## *Let's Pray*

Lord Jesus Christ, you are present in every page of the

Bible from beginning to end. Help us to see your presence and to appreciate the love that you pour out on us in every generation from age to age. Help us to accept the invitation you issue to join your battle for the hearts of humanity and to commit ourselves to loving service of one another. We ask this in the power of your Most Holy and Sacred Name. Amen.

## *What's Next?*

Now that we've got insight into Sacred Scripture and the story it tells us about love, we're going to explore the Sarraments and what they do to equip us to win the battle for love.

z

# CHAPTER 15. THE SACRAMENTS: EQUIPPING US TO WIN THE BATTLE FOR LOVE

## *Providing Supernatural Supports in Loving as Christ Loves*

*"I have a new commandment to give you, that you are to love one another; that your love for one another is to be like the love I have borne you." - John 13:34*

The Sacraments are supernatural signs of God's presence in the world which are made available to those who join the Catholic faith. The Catholic Church recognizes seven of them, all of which are designed to provide supernatural support in living out Christ's command to:

*"Love one another. As I have loved you, so you must love one another." - John 13:34*

Christ knew how difficult the choice to love one another is for us as human beings and knew we could not do it without His grace. The Church preserves the supports that Christ gave to us to help us in this quest to love:

- Baptism
- Confirmation
- The Eucharist
- Holy Orders

- Matrimony
- Confession
- Anointing of the Sick

Now that we know what Christ provided, and the Church preserves for us, let's explore what each Sacrament does for those who receive it.

## *Baptism: Armoring Our Hearts for Battle*

*"Amen, amen I say to thee, unless a man be born again of water and the Holy Ghost, he cannot enter into the kingdom of God." - John 3:5*

Everywhere around you, a great battle is being fought between love and its enemies. All people are conceived and born on this battlefield.

We cannot avoid this battle. Age is no protection against it. That battle begins in the womb. We are influenced by the outcome whether we wish to be or not.

When our mothers and fathers and people around us lose that battle and give into selfishness, our hearts get wounded. Those wounds make the choice for us to love others that much more difficult.

This is why all people - no matter their age - need Baptism. Baptism serves to heal the wounds received by those who bring their unarmored hearts into the Church and then armors them for the fight ahead so they take fewer hits and get wounded less often.

Baptism is one of the three sacraments of initiation, or entry into a life in Christ. During the ritual, water may be poured over the head of the candidate, or the candidate may be immersed, or plunged into the water.

*You know well enough that we who were taken up into Christ by baptism have been taken up, all of us, into his death. In our baptism, we have been buried with him, died like him, that so, just as Christ was raised up by his Father's power from the dead, we too might live and move in a new kind of existence. – Romans 6:3-4*

For more details about how baptism is performed, review the Catechism of the Catholic Church, Part Two, Section Two, Chapter 1, Article 1.

## *Confirmation: Equipping Us to Win the Fight*

In an ideal world, confirmation comes right after Baptism. It is an anointing with oil that marks the baptized person as belonging to Christ and infuses them with the Holy Spirit in a more direct way. It is also known as the laying on of hands.

*"On hearing this, they received baptism in the name of the Lord Jesus; and when Paul laid his hands upon them, the Holy Spirit came down on them, and they spoke with tongues, and prophesied." – Acts 19:5-6*

As a child makes choices in life, he enters into an internal battle between love and selfishness as well as an external battle to protect himself from the failures of others to love.

Confirmation equips a child for that battle by giving him 7 gifts that guide him in winning the battle for love with each decision he makes:

1. Knowledge: The ability to judge everything from a supernatural point of view, discerning right from wrong and good from evil

2. Wisdom: The ability to apply our knowledge of right and wrong and good and evil to our daily lives

3. Understanding: Supernatural insights into the meaning and purpose of revealed truths, which increases our trust in the Lord and our confidence in His word

4. Counsel: Enlightenment as to the right action to take, especially in difficult moments

5. Fortitude: The strength and willingness to sacrifice whatever must be sacrificed in order to carry out God's plan for our lives

6. Piety: A profound respect for God, a generous love for

him, and an affectionate obedience to all lawful authority

7. Fear of the Lord: A desire to protect our loving relationship with God at any cost such that we would do anything possible to avoid hurting that relationship or destroying it

In addition to these 7 gifts, we receive gifts specific to our particular purpose, or vocation, in life that to help us to live it.

*Now we have received not the spirit of the world, but the Spirit which is from God, that we might understand the gifts bestowed on us by God. - 1 Corinthians 2:12*

Now that we've explored what Confirmation brings us, let's examine what those gifts do to help us live out our call to love as Christ loves us.

## *Confirmation: Giving Us 7 Gifts of Love*

*"The spirit of the LORD shall rest upon him: a spirit of wisdom and of understanding, A spirit of counsel and of strength, a spirit of knowledge and of fear of the LORD." - Isaiah 11:2*

The 7 Gifts help us to:

- Know how to love
- Distinguish between real love and its counterfeits
- Understand what it means to love
- Choose the most loving action in every circumstance
- Be strong enough to love the unlovable and to choose love when we are most tempted to be selfish
- Desire love above all things
- Fear nothing except the loss of God's perfect love in our lives

Now that we understand how the 7 gifts of the Holy Spirit help us to live out the call to love as Christ loved, let's examine the role the Eucharist plays in helping us love one another.

## *The Eucharist: Keeping Us Nourished with Christ's Perfect Love*

The Eucharist is the living presence of Jesus Christ poured into bread and wine for the consumption of all those who believe in Him.

*"I am the living bread that came down from Heaven; whoever eats this bread will live forever; and the bread that I will give is my flesh for the life of the world." - John 6:51*

When we consume the Eucharist in a state of grace, where we've cleansed ourselves of sin and healed up the wounds so we can hold onto the love we receive, we are literally consuming the entire body, blood, soul, and divinity of Christ.

We are filling ourselves with His perfect love so we can share it with the world. Christ doesn't just give us help and support. He gives us HIMSELF in this sacrament so that we can love as He loves.

*"Whereupon Jesus said to them, Believe me when I tell you this; you can have no life in yourselves, unless you eat the flesh of the Son of Man, and drink his blood. The man who eats my flesh and drinks my blood enjoys eternal life, and I will raise him up at the last day. My flesh is real food, my blood is real drink. He who eats my flesh, and drinks my blood, lives continually in me, and I in him." - John 6:54-57*

In the Old Testament, the Israelites were instructed to sacrifice a lamb, mark the doorposts with its blood, and consume the entire thing as a sign they were part of the Covenant between God and the Children of Israel. Only if they did all three things could they be assured the angel of Death would pass over them.

*"The LORD said to Moses and Aaron in Egypt, "This month is to be for you the first month, the first month of your year. Tell the whole community of Israel that on the tenth day of this month each man is to take a lamb for his family, one for each household. If any household is too small for a whole lamb, they must share one with their nearest neighbor, having taken into account the number of people there are. You are to deter-*

*mine the amount of lamb needed in accordance with what each person will eat. The animals you choose must be year-old males without defect, and you may take them from the sheep or the goats. Take care of them until the fourteenth day of the month, when all the people of the community of Israel must slaughter them at twilight. Then they are to take some of the blood and put it on the sides and tops of the doorframes of the houses where they eat the lambs. That same night they are to eat the meat roasted over the fire, along with bitter herbs, and bread made without yeast. Do not eat the meat raw or cooked in water, but roast it over the fire--head, legs and inner parts. Do not leave any of it till morning; if some is left till morning, you must burn it. This is how you are to eat it: with your cloak tucked into your belt, your sandals on your feet and your staff in your hand. Eat it in haste; it is the LORD's Passover. "On that same night I will pass through Egypt and strike down every firstborn--both men and animals--and I will bring judgment on all the gods of Egypt. I am the LORD." The blood will be a sign for you on the houses where you are; and when I see the blood, I will pass over you. No destructive plague will touch you when I strike Egypt. "This is a day you are to commemorate; for the generations to come you shall celebrate it as a festival to the LORD--a lasting ordinance. – Exodus 12:1-14*

Each time that the Passover was celebrated, it was to be done in one house. No one who was a foreigner – someone outside the people of Israel – could partake of it.

*"The LORD said to Moses and Aaron, "These are the regulations for the Passover: "No foreigner is to eat of it. Any slave you have bought may eat of it after you have circumcised him, but a temporary resident and a hired worker may not eat of it. "It must be eaten inside one house; take none of the meat outside the house. Do not break any of the bones. The whole community of Israel must celebrate it." – Exodus 12:43-47*

In the Eucharist, Christ is our sacrificial lamb. We mark the door of our hearts with His blood, and we consume Him whole in the form of bread and wine. Thus, we can be assured protection from Death and will enter into eternal life. We eat it in the one house of the Lord: the Catholic Church, and the entire community gathers to partake of the meal. No one outside of the Catholic faith can be permitted to partake of it.

## *Confession: Healing the Wounds of Battle and Re-Equipping Us for the Fight*

Confession means going to a priest, entering into a designated area alone with him, and admitting to those moments when we've deliberately chosen to reject God's call to love.

*"With that, he breathed on them, and said to them, Receive the Holy Spirit; when you forgive men's sins, they are forgiven, when you hold them bound, they are held bound." - John 20: 22-23*

Every time we intentionally choose selfishness over love, we wound not only our own hearts but the hearts of those around us. We make it harder to choose love for ourselves and for others. We also wound Christ, whose sole desire for us is to love and be loved.

These wounds we open up, especially when they are the result of an intentional choice to do something we knew was not loving behavior, are all places where love leaks out of our hearts, preventing us from holding onto the love that gets poured into us by others.

We can be confident that Christ is present in the confessional because Christ promised us:

*"Where two or three are gathered together in my name, I am there in the midst of them." - Matthew 18:20*

The priest is not there to judge us or to condemn us. He is there in the person of Christ (in persona Christi) to facilitate an encounter with Christ. His role is to help us arrive at sincere repentance for our sins, clarity about the reason for those sins so that we might avoid the cause of them in the future, and to pass on Christ's words of forgiveness, healing, and love.

He also prescribes a penance for us - an act to perform that is an outward sign of our inward sorrow for having hurt God with our selfish behavior - which is designed to help us overcome the temptations that led to our failure in the future.

*"Confess your sins to one another, and pray for one another, for the healing of your souls. When a just man prays fervently, there is great virtue in his prayer." - James 5:16*

Armed with this understanding of confession's role in helping to heal the wounds of battle and re-equip us for the fight, mark this lesson complete. Let's see what the Anointing of the Sick does to help us win the battle for love.

## *Anointing of the Sick: Preparation for the Final Battle*

During the Anointing of the Sick, a priest is called who takes your confession and applies Sacred Oil to the head, the hands, and potentially the afflicted area in order to call down the healing power of the Holy Spirit.

*"Is any among you sick? Let him call for the elders of the church, and let them pray over him, anointing him with oil in the name of the Lord; and the prayer of faith will save the sick man, and the Lord will raise him up; and if he has committed sins, he will be forgiven" - James 5:14-15*

In the Anointing of the Sick, we ask for God's healing of our physical body if it is His will, but if not, we ask for His protection in the final hours of battle for our immortal souls. This final battle will be the toughest of our lives because the stakes are highest.

Our eternal life is at risk!

Now that we've examined what the Anointing of the Sick does for us, mark this lesson complete. Let's look at the Sacrament of Holy Orders to see what it does to help preserve love for all generations.

## *Holy Orders: Ensuring the Sacraments Remain Available for All Generations*

*"Presbyters who do their duty well should be considered deserving of a double honor, especially those who labor at preaching and teaching." - 1 Timothy 5:17*

Presbyters (meaning priests) and Bishops are appointed to keep the Church running and administer the Sacraments. This ensures all generations can access God's supernatural support in living out the call to love.

Only bishops can ordain priests and bishops. Only priests and bishops can turn ordinary bread and wine into the Body and Blood of Christ in the Eucharist, give confessions, or perform the Anointing of the Sick. These things are essential to helping us live out our call to love our neighbor as ourselves. Without priests, we lose the most essential Sacraments.

Scripture lays out strict requirements for the priesthood and the bishops:

*"If any one aspires to the office of bishop, he desires a noble task. Now a bishop must be above reproach, the husband of one wife, temperate, sensible, dignified, hospitable, an apt teacher, no drunkard, not violent but gentle, not quarrelsome and no lover of money. He must manage his own household well, keeping his children submissive and respectful in every way; for if a man does not know how to manage his own household, how can he care for God's church? He must not be a recent convert, or he may be puffed up in conceit and fall into the condemnation of the devil; moreover he must be well thought of by outsiders, or he may fall into reproach and the snares of the devil." – 1 Timothy 3:1-7*

The priesthood, and the office of bishop, have always been reserved for men alone. This is because the priest and bishop act as fathers to the congregation. Despite the confusion of the modern day, the reality is that only a man can be a father.

Christ came for the Jewish people. In order for them to recognize that He'd re-established the Davidic kingdom as promised, it needed to have all the right elements, including a male priesthood that made daily sacrifices in the temple. That's what priests and bishops do. They daily offer the sacrifice of the Mass for the faithful.

While it is true that in the earliest days priests and bishops were allowed to be married, by the Middle Ages, the Church determined that Paul's wisdom in calling for celibacy was great.

> *"The unmarried man is concerned about the work of the Lord, how he can please the Lord. But the married man is concerned about the affairs of this world, how he can please his wife." – 1 Cor. 7:32*

Thus, priests and bishops in the Roman Catholic Church are called to live in celibacy in the model of St. Joseph and St. Paul. Their lives are devoted entirely to the service of Christ's people,

> *"I wish you were all in the same state as myself; but each of us has his own endowment from God, one to live in this way, another in that."- 1 Corinthians 7:7*

It would be the cruelest thing to ask a man to choose between service to an earthly wife and earthly children and his service to Christ's Bride and Her children. Nor would that be fair to the wife or those children. She and those children would always, by necessity, play second fiddle to the Church.

His celibacy frees him from being forced to make a terrible choice between serving his family and serving the Church. It frees the woman he might marry and the children they might have from feeling like they are being neglected in favor of other people's families. It is a living sacrifice that he makes in imitation of Christ's sacrifice.

> *"The good shepherd lays down his life for the sheep." - John 10:11*

Now that we understand the role of the priesthood in keeping the sacraments available for all generations, mark this lesson complete. Let's talk about the role of Matrimony in raising up an army to fight the battle for love.

## *Matrimony: Raising Up an Army to Fight the Battle for Love*

> *"Has not the one God made you? You belong to Him in Body and Spirit. And what does the One God seek? Godly offspring. So be on your guard, and do not be unfaithful to the wife of your youth." – Micah 2:15*

God created marriage. His first commandment the man

and woman he made was:

*"Increase and multiply and fill the earth." – Genesis 1:26*

Marriage is a call to become a love generator. Married couples become living examples of Christ's unconditional love for His Church in two ways. First, in how they choose to love one another no matter what challenges confront their relationship. Second, in how they raise up and love the children that God sends their way.

They are called to generate more love by remaining open to life at all times. While a married couple may be physically unable to have children, they should remain open to the gift of new life in all acts of marital intimacy, trusting that if God chooses to bless them with a child, He will provide the means to care for that child.

Those who can't bear children of their own can still serve God by taking in children who have been orphaned, abandoned, abused, or neglected and teaching those children what it means to live in love. By modeling for those children what unconditional love for one another looks like when lived out daily, they help those children recognize genuine love and reject love's counterfeits.

In this way, they can raise an army of those who are ready to fight the battle for love in every generation. Now that we understand the role that matrimony plays in generating more love, let's engage in some exercises.

*"Go ye therefore, and teach all nations, baptizing them in the name of the Father, and of the Son, and of the Holy Ghost." – Matthew 28:19*

## *The Sacraments: Equipping Us to Win the Battle for Love Exercises*

Journal your answers to the following questions:

1. How did you see the sacraments before this lesson?

2. How do you see them now?

3. How do you feel about the gift you've received in these

sacraments of love?

4. What will you do to share this gift with others?

## *Let's Pray*

*Lord Jesus Christ, you gave us all the Great Commission to share your message of love with the world. Help us to take your message out in haste, with full faith that you will be with us and guide us every step of the way. Grant us the courage to speak truth in the face of hate and to love in the face of indifference. We ask this in the power of your Most Holy and Sacred Name. Amen.*

## *What's Next?*

Now that we understand more about what the Sacraments do to help us live out our call to love, let's explore the role of the Pope in helping us live lives of authentic love.

z

# CHAPTER 16. THE POPE: PRESERVING A PERFECT UNION OF LOVE

## *The Pope: Preserving Unity in the Church*

*"You are Peter, and upon this rock I will build my Church, and the gates of Hell will not prevail against it." - Matthew 16:18*

Jesus left us the first Pope, Peter, to act as a north star, pointing the Church toward love. That doesn't mean that everything Peter did was perfect. It wasn't.

*"But when Peter came to Antioch, I opposed him in public, because he was clearly wrong." - Galatians 2:11*

Paul called out Peter's behavior when Peter stopped eating with Gentile believers out of fear of the criticism of the Jewish believers, and by his actions, led others astray. He reminded Peter:

*"...that a person is put right with God only through faith in Christ, never by doing what the Law requires." - Galatians 2:16*

We know the Pope's behavior isn't guaranteed to be perfect. What is guaranteed is that when the Holy Spirit acts through him to make a definitive declaration about the direction the Church should go, we can trust that it's okay to follow Him.

This doctrine, known as Papal Infallibility, ensures that all believers are on the same page about what it means to give and receive love, and how to live out that call to love in every circumstance.

> *"There was one heart and soul in all the company of believers;"* - Acts 4: 32

Now that we understand what the doctrine of Papal infallibility guarantees and what it does not guarantee, let's examine some examples.

## *Thank the First Pope for Bacon!*

> *"...Peter went up to the house-top about noon, to pray there. He was hungry, and waiting for a meal; and while they were preparing it, he fell into a trance. He saw heaven opening, and a bundle, like a great sheet, let down by its four corners on to the earth; in it were all kinds of four-footed beasts, and things that creep on the earth, and all the birds of heaven. And a voice came to him, Rise up, Peter, lay about thee and eat. It cannot be, Lord, answered Peter; never in my life have I eaten anything profane, anything unclean. Then the voice came to him a second time, It is not for thee to call anything profane, which God has made clean. Three times this happened, and then the bundle was drawn up again into heaven."* - Acts 10:9-16

An example of Papal infallibility in action was Peter's early declaration - as a result of the actions of the Holy Spirit - that unclean meats were clean for all those baptized into Christ.

The meat of pigs was forbidden and considered unclean under the Old Covenant laws. If we didn't trust Peter's judgment on this, no Christian could enjoy a slice of bacon without sinning.

However, because of this promise from Christ, we can enjoy bacon without the guilt. This is also the reason most Easters are celebrated by serving ham. We celebrate Christ's fulfillment of the Old Covenant and His establishment of the New Covenant that frees us from those restrictions.

Now that we've explored this first example, let's look at examples of the special place Peter held in Christ's ministry.

## *The Special Role of Peter in Christ's Ministry*

In the Gospels, Peter is mentioned 191 times. The other 11 combined are mentioned 130. It is clear that Peter plays a prominent role in the story.

He features in more scenes. His name is always listed first among the apostles. Matthew even calls him the first, although in terms of the order in which they were called to Christ, Peter was not first.

*"These are the names of the twelve apostles; first, Simon, also called Peter," - Matthew 10:2*

Moreover, it was to Peter that the revelation of Christ as Lord was made known.

*"Simon Peter answered, "You are the Messiah, the Son of the living God." - Matthew 16:16*

It is to Peter that Christ says:

*"I will give you the keys of the kingdom of heaven; whatever you bind on earth will be bound in heaven, and whatever you loose on earth will be loosed in heaven." - Matthew 16: 19*

This demonstrates the special place that Peter held both with Christ and the other apostles. Now that we understand how important Peter was considered to be, let's discuss the Pope and his connection to Peter.

## *The Pope: Successor to Peter*

Peter, before his death in 67 A.D., passed on his legacy to Linus. According to the historical writings of Eusebius, the Linus who became the Pope after St. Peter is the same mentioned by Paul in 2 Timothy 4:21:

*"Make haste, and come to me before winter. ...Eubulus and Pudens and Linus and Claudia and all the brethren send thee their greeting."*

Paul was in Rome at the time, awaiting his death. Linus held the Papal office for eight years, from 67 A.D. to 76 A.D. When he died, that office passed to Anacletus, who held it from 79 A.D. to 92 A.D. After Anacletus came Clement I, from 88 to

99 A.D. After Clement I came Evaristus from 99 to 107 A.D. After him came Alexander I, from 107- 115 A.D. After Alexander I came Sixtus I from 115 - 124 A.D.

After Sixtus I came Telesphorus from 126-136 A.D., followed by Hyginus from 136-142 A.D.. After that came Pius I from 140-154, Anicetus from 157-168 A.D., Soter from 167-174 A.D., Eleuterus from 174-189 A.D., Victor I from 189-199 A.D., Zephyrinus from 199-217 A.D., Callixtus I from 218-222 A.D., Urban I from 222-230 A.D., Pontian from 230-235 A.D., Anterus from 235-236 A.D., Fabian from 236-250 A.D., Cornelius from 251-253 A.D., Lucius I from 253-254 A.D., Stephen I from 254-257 A.D.

After Stephen I came Sixtus II from 257-258 A.D., Dionysus from 259-268 A.D., Felix I from 269-274 A.D., Eutychian from 275-283 ad, Caius from 283-296 A.D., Marcellinus from 296-304 A.D., Marcellus I from 308-309 A.D., Eusebius from 310-310 A.D., Miltiades from 311-314 A.D..

It was in the time of Miltiades that Emperor Constantine issued the Edict of Milan, decriminalizing Christianity and decreeing that Roman citizens had "the liberty to observe the religion of their choice and their particular mode of worship."

Sylvester I from 314-335 A.D. During Sylvester's Papacy, the first council of Nicaea was held which confirmed Christ as both divine and human.

Mark from 336-336 A.D., Julius I from 337-352 A.D., Liberius from 352-366 A.D., Damasus I from 366-384 A.D., Siricius from 384-399 A.D., Anastasius I from 399-401 A.D., Innocent I from 401-417 A.D., Zosimus I from 417-418 A.D., Boniface I from 418-422 A.D., Celestine I from 422-432 A.D., Sixtus III from 432-440 A.D., Leo I from 400-461.

Leo I provided a precise, systematic doctrine of Christ's Incarnation and the hypostatic union of both of his natures called The Tome. Leo I was instrumental in persuading the Huns not to attack Rome in 452 and the Vandals not to sack Rome in 455. He is a doctor of the Church, as declared by Pope Benedict XVI in 1754.

You can explore the full line of succession that leads us to

Pope Francis I, our current pope at the time of creation of this resource, by visiting this site: https://popehistory.com/popes/

This unbroken lineage ensures that what Christ handed on to Peter is passed on to each generation and is not lost to believers. Now that we understand the role of Papal Succession, mark this lesson complete. Let's examine the role the Pope plays in providing clarity about how to apply God's laws to everyday life.

## *The Pope: Providing Clarity on Catholic Beliefs*

There's a joke in the Jewish faith. Ask two Rabbis for an answer on any subject, and you'll get three opinions. Debate and discussion are corner stones of the Jewish culture and part of their quest for the Truth.

As good as that is, this means there is no one to provide definitive answers about how to apply the laws of God to everyday life when hard questions arise. This is because there is no one person possessing the authority to give a final yes or no.

If there is no one to give a final yes or not, there is no final yes or no. Everything remains open to debate and discussion.

Debate and discussion are good things, but are limited to human understanding. Christ understood this, which is why He provides divine guidance through the Pope, who is given the ability to say a definitive yes or no to any doctrine.

Scripture does not and cannot address every issue that comes up. There must be someone to guide the faithful in the right things to do as situations arise. That clarity comes from the Pope.

Now that we understand the clarity provided by the pope and its help in guiding us toward living lives of authentic love, let's examine the role the Holy Spirit plays in choosing the Pope.

## *The Holy Spirit: Guiding the Pope's Selection*

We don't deny that the Pope is a man. He is selected by other men.

How can we trust, then, that the right man is being selected for the job?

We trust in Christ's promises that the Gates of Hell will not prevail against His Church. We trust that the one chosen to lead the Church is the one the Holy Spirit knows we need for the times we face.

Whether we find the Pope to be easy to love or hard to love, we submit ourselves to the authority of the Pope as an act of submission to God's will for His Church.

*"The Lord loves obedience better than any sacrifice, the attentive ear better than the fat of rams." - 1 Samuel 15:22*

We know that no matter how men might conspire to work against God's plan, God will work all of their plans for our ultimate good and His glory.

*"Meanwhile, we are well assured that everything helps to secure the good of those who love God, those whom he has called in fulfilment of his design." - Romans 8:28*

Now that we know how we can be confident that the right man is selected for Pope each time, it's time to engage in some exercises.

## *Exercises*

Journal your answers to the following questions:

1. What did I believe about the Pope before this lesson?

2. What do I believe about it now?

3. If my beliefs have changed, how am I going to live this belief moving forward?

4. What will I do to help those who struggle with this belief?

## *Let's Pray*

Lord Jesus Christ, you provided the office of the Pope to keep us united in you. Please help us to embrace the leadership and authority the office represents and to pray at all times for the man who holds that office. When we are tempted to complain or to criticize, may we instead seek your wisdom and guidance in how to be a solution to the problems we see. We ask all this in the power of your most Holy and Sacred Name. Amen.

## *What's Next?*

Now that we've discussed the role of the Pope in preserving a perfect union of love, let's talk about the community of believers and how important that is to helping us practice our skills in love.

z

# CHAPTER 17. THE COMMUNITY OF BELIEVERS: PRACTICING LOVE

## *The Community: Christ's Body*

*"And you are Christ's body, organs of it depending upon each other." - 1 Corinthians 12:27*

Mass is a gathering of Catholic believers, led by the priest, who join to celebrate the Eucharistic feast. Daily masses are held at many parishes, but all Catholics are required to attend weekly Mass on Sundays and Holy Days of Obligation. These Holy Days of Obligation are set by the Church as feast days to honor the Lord in a special way for a special purpose.

During Mass, we enter into Heaven for an hour. We hear the Word of God and we are nourished with Christ's Body, Blood, Soul, and Divinity. Then, we are sent back out into the world to share the love of Christ with others.

## *Learning to Function as One Body in Christ*

But attending Mass on Sundays is not enough to help us grow in our capacity to give and receive love. We need help practicing the skills required to love in an environment, especially practicing our ability to forgive others their mistakes and to allow ourselves to be forgiven for our own mistakes. This is why we need to be an active part of the community of believers.

That means volunteering to be part of the Church's ministries, working together to serve outside of the Church, and coming together to study the Word and encourage one another to put it into practice. If your faith begins and ends at the Church doors, you're missing 99% of what you're meant to be getting in instruction in how to give and receive love.

*"...just so we, though many in number, form one body in Christ, and each acts as the counterpart of another." - Romans 12:5*

As a Protestant friend of mine put it, "Being part of the community outside the church, that's where it really matters. That's where real life goes down. It's easy to be saved in church. It's the fellowship and encounters outside the four walls – not the two hours a week in Church – where we put into practice what we learn during those two hours. That's where we demonstrate the authentic love. Too many people know how to "act" in church, but don't put love into action outside of the Church walls."

*"But be doers of the word, and not hearers only, deceiving yourselves." – James 1:22*

She may not be Catholic yet, but she understands the heart of the matter. Mass is where we hear and receive the Words of love. Community is our chance to be doers of the Word also, putting our love into action on behalf of one another.

Now that we understand why we must be an active part of Christ's community of believers, let's look at what else happens when we are part of the life of the community.

## *Community: Serving and Being Served*

*"Love cannot remain by itself - it has no meaning. Love has to be put into action, and that action is service." - Blessed Mother Teresa of Calcutta*

Participating in the life of the community takes the Church beyond being a place where "everybody knows your name and they're always glad you came," - a line from the sit-com Cheers theme song - to being a family.

Here, we serve one another and we are served in return.

Here, we work together to care for each other's needs. We extend the love to our surrounding communities, pooling our resources and giving of our time to serve those in need.

*"Be affectionate towards each other, as the love of brothers demands, eager to give one another precedence. I would see you unwearied in activity, aglow with the Spirit, waiting like slaves upon the Lord; buoyed up by hope, patient in affliction, persevering in prayer; providing generously for the needs of the saints, giving the stranger a loving welcome." - Romans 12:10-13*

Now that we've unlocked the role that service within the community plays in helping us grow in love, let's talk about the realities of being part of a community.

## *The Church: A Hospital for Sinners and a Training Ground for Saints*

*"Forgiveness is the restoration of freedom to oneself; it is the key held in our hand to our prison cell." - St. John Paul the Great*

If you're going to step up and become part of any community, especially a community of believers in Christ, you need to understand that you are going to get hurt. Not once, but often. It won't always happen by intention. Most of the time it will come through miscommunication and misunderstanding.

Sometimes it will come because someone is choosing the wrong way to try and help themselves feel better about life, and you end up being collateral damage. They didn't intend to hurt you. They just wanted to do something to make themselves feel better.

Every human relationship by default comes with both the cross and the crucifixion as well as the glory and the resurrection. You won't get to the glory and the resurrection of a relationship unless you can endure the pain of the cross and crucifixion moments.

The Church's role is not to be a shrine for saints. We don't go there to find people who are perfected in love. We go there because we need to be perfected in love.

The Church is a hospital for sinners, treating each person and meeting them where they are. Some are deep wells of love, some can barely hold a thimbleful of it. All of us are seeking to grow in that capacity.

It is also a place of learning, helping us to develop the skills needed to grow in our capacity to give and receive love. We will all need to be forgiven at some point in time, just as we will all need to forgive one another at some point in time. Those who cannot forgive are rejecting God's love and rejecting His forgiveness not only for themselves but for others.

We're being trained to love the unlovable in the world by how we love those around us in the Church. The world may not forgive us for our mistakes, but our brothers and sisters in Christ are being trained in how to do that work. They may struggle, just as we may, with it.

In order to belong somewhere...we must be long in that place...long past the point where we get hurt and must choose to forgive to remain part of things. If we can't forgive, we place walls between our heart and the hearts of others that block the love from reaching us.

Now that we know what to expect when we become part of the Church's community of believers, let's talk about the role that community plays in helping us find our purpose.

## *The Community: Helping Us Find and Live Our Purpose*

Every Catholic Church is granted responsibility to care for those who live within a pre-defined territory. Those territories are known as a parish. Those who live within these boundaries should be attending that church.

We aren't meant to "shop" for a Church that fits us. We attend that Church to meet Christ. If the Church is empty in some area, as the wine jugs were at the wedding Jesus attended, we should follow Mary's example. First, bring it to Jesus. Second, do whatever He tells us to do. It could be God brought us there to fill that gap!

We are all pieces in God's jigsaw puzzle of love. Each of us plays an important role. None of us can be discarded without leaving a gap that will need to be filled.

It's not until we connect to a community that our unique shape makes sense. The way we were formed and the tendencies that come naturally to us begin to make sense here. Even our weaknesses serve a purpose in the community.

Our strengths allow us a place to shine as we serve and support the other members in their weaknesses. Our weaknesses provide others with room to shine as they serve and support us. Nothing about you is accidental. Nothing about you is incidental.

It's all part of God's plan to fill the needs of His people. The more that you step up to serve in your parish community, the more that your purpose and the unique way that you are meant to fulfill that purpose will become clear to you.

*"And let us consider how to stir up one another to love and good works, not neglecting to meet together, as is the habit of some, but encouraging one another , and all the more as you see the Day draw near." - Hebrews 10:24-25*

## *The Parish Community and the Family: Training Grounds for Love*

The family is meant to be the first training ground for love, with the father and mother working together to provide that daily example of love in action. However, when the family fails, the parish community is meant to pick up the slack and expand on what was learned in the home.

As Catholics, we are part of Christ's army, fighting a daily battle for love. It is in our service to each other in the parish and through participation in her ministries and various activities that we are given the opportunity to learn and practice our skills in love.

The Mass is the mess hall. We're there to be fed and nurtured, and our focus should be on Christ while we are at

Mass. He's the centerpiece and highlight of the event.

The various ministries, classes, and activities put on by the Church are our opportunity to connect with one another and practice the skills required to grow in love.

Once we leave the Church grounds, though, this love should not stop. We need to be taking it out into the world and sharing it with people whose only Gospel may be their encounter with you!

## *Exercises*

Journal your answers to the following questions:

1. Are you part of a parish community?

2. If not, will you seek to become part of one?

3. If not, why not?

4. Have you been hurt while part of a community?

5. If so, have you forgiven those who hurt you?

6. If not, what's stopping you?

7. If you've not forgiven those who hurt you, have you allowed that pain to keep you from the community?

8. If you're struggling to forgive, ask God to help you see the situation as He does and find forgiveness for those who have wounded you so they don't keep you from receiving the love He wants you to receive.

9. Now that you've completed this lesson, have you reconsidered your decision?

## *Let's Pray*

Heavenly Father, you created us to live in communion with one another. Lord Jesus Christ, you invite us all to be part of your body, a communion of believers. Holy Spirit, you show us the way to forgive and to heal from our wounds, to allow us to forgive and to help others heal. Please reveal to me any obstacles that I face in becoming part of the community of believers that I might bring it to Christ and ask Him to either remove the obstacle or heal the wound, so that I may fill my cup of love to overflowing and allow it to spill out onto all those around me. I ask all this in the power of the Most Sacred Name of our Lord Jesus Christ. Amen.

## *What's Next?*

Now that we've got a better understanding of the role the community plays in helping us live in love, let's talk about what role the laws and precepts of the Church play in that same thing.

z

# CHAPTER 18. LIVING IN LOVE: THE LAWS AND THE PRE- CEPTS OF THE CHURCH

## *The Two Greatest Commandments*

*"Master, which commandment in the law is the greatest? Jesus said to him, Thou shalt love the Lord thy God with thy whole heart and thy whole soul and thy whole mind. This is the greatest of the commandments, and the first. And the second, its like, is this, Thou shalt love thy neighbour as thyself. On these two commandments, all the law and the prophets depend." - Matthew 22:36-40*

Everything the Catholic Church teaches, preaches, does, and requires of its members is designed to help you live out these particular two commandments. If you ever find yourself becoming overwhelmed by the number of things Catholics must do to remain faithful to the Church, just bring yourself back to this.

Let's talk, though, about what Christ and the Church mean by the word "love." It's an easy word to manipulate and many people use it to describe many different things. Here, though, when we speak about love we are NOT describing an emotion. The emotion may lend itself to the action, but for Catholics, love is an ACTION.

*"My little children, let us shew our love by the true test of action, not by taking phrases on our lips." - 1 John 3:18*

Christ didn't just talk about wanting to save us. He took action to save us.

*"God has proved his love to us by laying down his life for our sakes; we too must be ready to lay down our lives for the sake of our brethren." - 1 John 3:16*

Now that we know what Christ - and the Church - mean by love, and what the two greatest commandments are, let's talk about the ten commandments and how those guide us in living lives of love.

## *The Ten Commandments of Love*

Many people question the necessity of following the 10 commandments. Aren't they Old Testament and we are a New Testament people?

However, if we examine them through the lens of love, we will discover the role they play in helping to make sure we are living lives of authentic love.

The first three Commandments deal with our relationship with God, who is love itself:

1. I, the Lord, am your God. You shall not have any other gods beside me.

2. You shall not take the name of the Lord, your God, in vain.

3. Remember to keep Holy the Sabbath day.

The singular message of these is:

1. Make love your first priority, as it is what makes life worth living.

2. Don't call actions and behaviors that are not loving (actions of self-sacrifice for another's greater good) by the name of love.

3. Set apart Sundays for gathering together to spread love to one and all. Getting our cup of love refilled at least once each week is critical to being able to give love to others.

Why Sunday rather than Saturday, as the traditional Sabbath is celebrated? Because Sunday is the day the New Covenant was established through Christ's Resurrection. On that day, He made everything new.

The next seven Commandments deal with how we are to treat our neighbor:

## 4. Honor your father and mother.

This is a hard commandment for many who have suffered abuse at the hands of their parents. However, by honoring our father and mother, we are honoring the parts of ourselves that come from them. It is a way of showing respect for ourselves to show respect to them.

This commandment isn't limited to our immediate father and mother. It's really about honoring all of those who came before us and contributed to shaping and forming us into the people we are today.

## 5. You shall not murder.

Without the right to life, no other right matters. You won't exist to care about other rights. Life is necessary for human love to exist.

Therefore, to protect love, human life must be safeguarded and protected. While it may be necessary to take a human life to protect and defend the lives of others, this is not the preferred option.

## 6. You shall not commit adultery.

Marriage is meant to be a living symbol of God's unconditional love. When we commit adultery, we are hurting other people's ability to trust in God's unconditional love and to experience it for themselves. We sacrifice love on the altar of our selfishness, pride, and vanity.

## 7. You shall not steal.

Trust is essential to love. When we steal, we undermine the trust people have in us and in one another. We make it more difficult for people to be generous and trusting.

## 8. You shall not bear false witness against your neighbor.

Honesty is essential for love to flourish and thrive. If you can't be honest about who you are, where you are, exactly as you are - how can anyone love you there? Furthermore, when we lie and deceive with the intention of doing harm to another, we are destroying their relationships and their ability to give and receive love. We may even be endangering their lives.

### 9. You shall not covet your neighbor's wife.

Coveting means to actively entertain thoughts of being with or possessing that wife (or husband). By choosing to engage in such thoughts, we create barriers to us being able to truly love the neighbor or their spouse. We begin to see the spouse we're coveting as an object, not a person, and the neighbor as an obstacle to our own desires and happiness.

### 10. You shall not covet anything that belongs to your neighbor.

As stated earlier, when we covet, we create barriers to being able to love our neighbor as ourselves. We see the things that belong to our neighbor as being more important to us than the neighbor.

Now that we've explored the ten commandments and how they help guide us in living out lives of love, mark this lesson complete. Let's examine the 8 Beatitudes of love, hope, and joy.

## *The 8 Beatitudes of Love, Hope, and Joy*

The beatitudes are eight solemn blessings which mark the opening of Jesus's Sermon on the Mount. Delivered in Matthew 5:3-10, they form a beautiful picture of the ideal for Christian living.

1. Blessed are the poor in spirit, for theirs is the kingdom of Heaven.
2. Blessed are the meek, for they will inherit the earth.
3. Blessed are they who mourn: for they shall be comforted.
4. Blessed are those who hunger and thirst for righteousness, for they will be filled.
5. Blessed are the merciful, for they will receive mercy.

6. Blessed are the pure in heart, for they will see God.

7. Blessed are the peacemakers, for they will be called children of God.

8. Blessed are those who are persecuted for righteousness' sake, for theirs is the Kingdom of Heaven.

When we are poor in spirit, we look at love as our greatest wealth and put everything we have in the service of it. We prioritize love before any other material good or physical relationship.

When we are meek, we choose to prioritize our relationships and seek to foster those above everything else.

We only mourn when we lose something we love deeply, so being able to mourn means that we've loved others. When we mourn for those we love, we can be assured that God will comfort us by restoring them to us in the fullness of time.

Righteousness means right living, or living a life dedicated to love. When we hunger and thirst for that, we will do everything in our power to spread love to others and to be an example of it.

When we show mercy to others, forgiving and bearing wrongs patiently, we keep our hearts open to love and we can be sure that we will receive a full measure of it poured back into us.

The pure in heart are continually cleansing themselves of all those things that block the flow of love in their lives. They work hard to remove every hint of hardness of heart that stems from unforgiveness and to bring to Christ every wound that diminishes their capacity to give and receive love. They examine themselves on a regular basis to be sure they stay open to love and to operating with love.

The peacemakers are always looking for opportunities to help people mend their relationships with each other and with God. They leverage their relationship with love to help prevent miscommunications and smooth out misunderstandings, looking for ways to restore the flow of love wherever they see it being blocked.

Finally, we come to those who endure all manner of mockery, abuse, rejection, and difficulty caused by their decision to take a stand and defend authentic love from its counterfeits. They will experience the fullness of love on Earth and in eternity.

Now that we see what the Beatitudes do to help us experience love, hope, and joy, let's go over the Apostle's Creed and its guidance in what we believe as those who embrace the fullness of Christ's teachings.

## *The Apostle's Creed: Embracing the Hope of Love Everlasting*

The Apostle's Creed is a concise summary of all that we, in the Catholic faith, believe and teach. The Apostle's Creed predates the Council of Nicea in 385 and is believed to be the oldest creed.

According to tradition, each one of the twelve apostles contributed an article to it under the guidance of the Holy Spirit, hence why it is called The Apostle's Creed. It is believed to have been first written down sometime in the second century A.D.

It can be a challenge to recite for those who do not claim Catholicism as their faith or for those who do not believe in God. But it need not be a stumbling block to those who pursue love if you look at it as a super condensed story containing important truths about love.

Reciting the words frequently commits that story to memory and allows us to call it to mind during moments when the decision to love is especially difficult. We can also recite it when we face deep discouragement and the temptation to quit on our journey to love. We do not have to believe the story is literal truth in order to gain the benefit, we need only to believe in the message behind the story.

In the next few sections, I will break down, statement by statement, how it relates to love and to helping you live out the call to love in your daily life.

## I believe in God, the Father Almighty

*"for God is love"* – *1 John 4:8*

We begin with this statement to acknowledge that love, who is God, is the supreme force that guides our lives and the purpose for which we live it. Love is the heart of the story we are about to tell, and love is the reason for its existence. Everything we choose to do is to be guided by love if we are to find, and cling to, authentic hope and joy.

## Creator of Heaven and Earth

*"In the beginning, God created the heavens and the earth"*
*– Genesis 1:1*

We acknowledge that love is what brought us, and all things, into being both the perfect and the imperfect. Love brought us into this world that we might grow in love and one day reach perfection in it.

## And in Jesus Christ, His only Son, our Lord

*"You shall call his name Jesus, He will be great, and will be called Son of the Most High...and he will reign over the house of Jacob forever and of His kingdom there will be no end"* – *Luke 1:31-33*

In this statement, we embrace an incredible and powerful idea: That same love that created us and all things, in its full power and majesty, came to earth not merely to temporarily take our form but to become one of us. We accept the leadership of God made man, Love Incarnate, who was named Jesus. We agree to take up His quest to love our fellow human beings as He did.

## Who was conceived by the Holy Spirit

*And the angel said to her, "The Holy Spirit will come upon you and the power of the Most High will overshadow you, therefore the child to be born will be called holy, the Son of God"* – *Luke 1:35*

God, who is Love, was not content to allow humanity to struggle and to suffer without guidance. Love took action, and that is what we are required to do as well. Love acted on behalf of humanity by seeking out a young woman who would be willing to cooperate with Him in His quest to show humanity by example what it meant to love their neighbors as themselves.

## **Born of the Virgin Mary**

Love could not become truly human without the consent of a woman. His very nature would not allow Him to force her cooperation. She had to consent.

Anything else He could have done on His own, but for this to work, He didn't want to just take on the appearance of humanity – he wanted to go through the experience of being human from conception through death. He needed to live it so that He could see first-hand what it meant to be human and show us, by His lived example, how to live out the call to love from beginning to end.

Mary believed in love, and she consented to cooperate with Him in His mission. She allowed love to be conceived in her womb and born from her body. And she mothered Him as any mother would – patiently, tenderly caring for His many needs as He grew.

This partnership with love allowed the two of them to do greater things than either of them could have accomplished on their own. Without humanity's cooperation, love could never have become truly one of us.

Without love's help, Mary could never have raised their son to become the perfect example of a life lived in love that humanity needed. Love made sure she had all that she needed to be able to raise their son to be the example of love the plan would require, protecting her from the stain of sin of any kind.

## **Suffered under Pontius Pilate, was crucified, died, and was buried.**

*"Then Pilate took Jesus and scourged him." – John 19:1*

*"When the soldiers had crucified Jesus, they took his garments," – John 19:23*

*"When Jesus had received the vinegar, he said, 'It is finished' and he bowed his head and gave up his spirit" – John 19:30*

*"They took the body of Jesus, and bound it in linen cloths*

*with the spices, as is the burial custom of the Jews...since the tomb was nearby, they laid Jesus there." – John 19:40, 42*

In the middle of what has thus far been a beautiful story about love seeing the needs of humanity and being motivated to take action in cooperation with Mary to solve the problem comes a grim reminder of the realities of choosing this path. Love did not spare the Son He created nor will love spare us from the pain, suffering, and death we will experience as we walk the path of love.

Jesus did not have to die. He had the power to break free of His bonds at any time. He chose it so that man would know how to love.

It was important to the crucifixion's meaning that the betrayal happened at the hands of all, but especially at the hands of His own. Judas betrayed Him and Peter abandoned Him. His own people chose to free a murderer rather than let Him go.

He died for every single one of those people, the ones who stuck by His side and the ones who betrayed Him, the ones who spat on Him and the ones who scourged Him, the ones who turned away and washed their hands of Him, and the ones who turned away and watched, doing nothing, as it happened.

Some of His final words were,

*"Father, forgive them, for they know not what they do." – Luke 23:34*

Sometimes, love hurts. Loving other people will not always lead to being loved in return. Sometimes it will lead to being hurt emotionally, physically, or mentally. We must love them enough to die for them anyway. We must love them enough to forgive them no matter how deep a pain they cause us, and to love them past their unlovable behavior.

Walking the path of love and following its ways, does not lead us to an easy life. There will be suffering, there will be false judgments, there will be pain, there will be loss, and there will be times when it seems that it was all for nothing and hate has won. But that doesn't mean the journey isn't worth it in the end.

## He descended into Hell

> *For Christ also died for sins once for all, the just for the unjust, so that He might bring us to God, having been put to death in the flesh, but made alive in the spirit; in which also He went and made proclamation to the spirits now in prison, who once were disobedient. – 1 Peter 3:18-20*

At this moment when all seems lost will come the final confrontation. It is this moment that everything we've been doing has been leading us toward. Jesus didn't have to go to Hell. He went, as we learn in 1 Peter 3, to free all those who were held captive by their past by offering them the chance to join Him.

Jesus, the embodiment of Perfect love, died. However, His power continued to act on behalf of all of humanity. This story reminds us that although love may appear to die, it is never truly dead. Even in death, love's power continues to act in secret, unseen by the eyes of men, to rescue those who are imprisoned by pain or grief or sorrow or anger.

## And on the third day

> *In their fright the women bowed down with their faces to the ground, but the men said to them, "Why do you look for the living among the dead? He is not here; he has risen! Remember how he told you, while he was still with you in Galilee: 'The Son of Man must be delivered over to the hands of sinners, be crucified and on the third day be raised again.' " Then they remembered his words. – Luke 24:5-8*

This final confrontation may seem to last forever, but its time is limited and will end. It is during this time that we rely on this story to provide us with real hope – the hope that things will, if we hang on, turn around and we will see love's triumph.

## He rose again from the dead

> *"But now Christ has been raised from the dead, the first fruits of those who are asleep. For since by a man came death, by a man also came the resurrection of the dead. For as in Adam all die, so also in Christ all will be made alive." – 1 Corinthians 15:20-23*

Love will triumph in the end. The pain, the suffering, the anguish, even the death we may suffer will not extinguish it. Everything we go through will be worth it in the end. And this story reminds us of that.

If we do not give up, if we persevere and push forward, love will triumph and come back to life more powerful than it ever was.

## He ascended into Heaven

*Now when He had spoken these things, while they watched, He was taken up, and a cloud received Him out of their sight. And while they looked steadfastly toward heaven as He went up, behold, two men stood by them in white apparel, who also said, "Men of Galilee, why do you stand gazing up into heaven? This same Jesus, who was taken up from you into heaven, will so come in like manner as you saw Him go into heaven." - Acts 1:9-12*

This story includes a promise: there is something greater than what earth has to offer and we can ascend to it. We can attain perfection in love, and when we live in love perfectly, which is what Heaven is, we will experience a fullness of peace, a complete and perfect joy, and hope that never diminishes for it is replenished continuously by the presence of love in our lives. It will raise us up.

## Is seated at the right hand of God, the Father Almighty

To sit at the right hand of a ruler was a sign that the leader both honored, respected, and trusted you. It was to allow you a share in that leadership.

When we allow love to reign over our lives, we will attain the respect and honor of others and the blessings which love has to offer will be ours to command.

## From thence He shall come to judge the living and the dead

This part of the story reminds us that our time to choose to live a life of love expires at the end of our life. We will be eternally judged by the rest of humanity by the choices and decisions we make today. It is up to us to choose our path.

## I believe in the Holy Spirit

Love is not a passive force. It acts. The Holy Spirit is that motivation and drive to act on love's behalf, even and especially when it requires great risk to ourselves and those to whom we are close.

## The Holy Catholic Church

The Holy Catholic Church is, in the story of the Apostle's Creed, a body of people united in the service of love. All those who gather together in the name of love and who commit themselves to not only following the path of love Incarnate but to helping others do the same make themselves members of the Body of love made man and are sanctified – set apart – (Holy) for the purpose of love are gathered in unity (the word Catholic means universal) in the Lord's house (the word Church means Lord's house).

We are called to join together by the example of love, who joined together with Mary to accomplish together what they could not accomplish alone. Humanity needed a savior, Mary didn't have the ability to save them. Humanity needed someone among them to be an example of what living in love really looked like, and love wasn't able to give them that alone. Together, they were able to accomplish the salvation of man where neither of them could have alone.

Love could have accomplished salvation another way, if Mary proved unwilling, but this was the best way – the one that would save the most souls and rescue the most people.

## The Communion of Saints

*Therefore, since we are surrounded by such a great cloud of witnesses, let us throw off everything that hinders and the sin that so easily entangles. And let us run with perseverance the race marked out for us, - Hebrews 12:1*

Saints are all those of the past, present, and future whose lives are devoted to love and who continue to offer their guidance and wisdom by their example as we seek to walk this path.

Some commonly known saints are St. Peter, St. Paul, St.

Matthew, St. John the Apostle, St. Francis of Assisi, and Joan of Arc. Though their bodies may die, those souls who die in the arms of Christ live on in Him and are able to continue acting – through Him - to help us.

## The Forgiveness of Sins

Sin is a failure to love, but it is also an opportunity to learn more about love and to see where we still need to grow in our capacity to love. Life is a study in love, and we will each fail many, many times and many different ways before we are able to finally fully understand what it is to love.

Forgiveness for these failures, both our own and those of others, is an essential ingredient to our ability to grow in love. We are encouraged to look with compassion on those who have fallen in their walk, and to try and lift them up and encourage them to try again even as we work to help them understand what caused them to stumble. In turn, they do the same for us.

## The Resurrection of the Body

This portion of the story may be hard for an atheist to believe, let alone to say, but bear with me. In reminding ourselves of the resurrection to come, we are reminding ourselves that every death brings new life. Everything that has been lost to us because we chose the path of love will be restored to us in a more perfect form when love reigns supreme.

The body dies to become new life in the plant that grows. The plant dies to become new life in the deer that grazes. The deer dies to become new life in the bear that eats it. All death brings new life, and that includes the death of our hopes and dreams.

## And Life Everlasting

In this final statement, we are reminded that eventually all things pass away, but love never dies. As long as we live in love, our lives continue, too.

Having fully examined the Apostles Creed and its lessons on love, let's mark this lesson complete. It's time to explore the 5 Precepts and the Defined Dogmas of the Church and its relationship to love.

## The 5 Precepts of the Church and the Defined Dogmas

The Precepts of the Catholic Church are the actions required for all those who want to live in the fullness of God's love:

The five precepts of the Catholic Church are:

1. Attend Mass on Sundays and days of obligation

2. Confess your sins at least once a year

3. Receive the Eucharist at least once a year

4. Observe days of fasting and abstinence

5. Provide for the needs of the Church

We'll talk more about what Mass does for us in the next lesson, but attending Mass fills us up with God's love and sends us out into the world prepared to share it with others. That's why it's a requirements to live in the fullness of love.

Confessing our sins heals the wounds and removes the blockages that are preventing us from being able to give and receive love to our maximum capacity. It's hard to love. Requiring confession at least once a year ensures that we're getting the help we need to do it well.

Receiving the Eucharist at least once a year is designed to keep our hearts filled up with Christ's love and capable of giving it out to others. It's the literal bare minimum, though. You're not going to be strong enough to fight battles effectively if you're only eating once a year!

The days of fasting and abstinence set by the Church are there to get us to focus on growing in love. We deliberately and intentionally say no to the body's desires to meet our physical needs, focusing instead on practices that help us grow our heart's capacity to give and receive love such as almsgiving and service to others. This helps us conquer our natural tendency to prioritize our physical desires above love's needs.

*"Only it is to be a free offering, not a grudging tribute. I would remind you of this, He who sows sparingly will reap sparingly; he who sows freely will reap freely too. Each of you*

*should carry out the purpose he has formed in his heart, not with any painful effort; it is the cheerful giver God loves." – 2 Corinthians 9:5-7*

Providing for the needs of the Church by giving of our time, talents, and treasure according to our means helps there to be a place for people to go and learn about love. It ensures that the Church can continue to be a visible presence in the world and a physical reminder of God's love for all of humanity.

We must also accept as true all the defined Dogmas of the Catholic Church. These are based on revealed truths of Jesus Christ and the Holy Spirit throughout the ages. We've covered many of them in detail already. All of them are important for helping us know what it is God requires for us to live in the fullness of His love.

Now that you understand what the 5 Precepts of the Catholic Church and her defined dogmas do to help us live in love, it's time to engage in our exercises.

## *Exercises*

Journal your answers to the following questions:

1. Do I see how all the laws, the commandments, and the Church's precepts help me to live a life of authentic love?

2. If not, which part of it confuses me or causes me to disagree?

3. Have I prayed over this part and asked for the Holy Spirit to guide me to the truth?

4. If not, why not?

5. If I do see how it all contributes to living a life of authentic love, what do I plan to do with that insight? How will it change how I live today?

## *Let's Pray*

Holy Spirit, you guide and direct us to operate in obedience with the Church and Her teachings. Help me to open my eyes and my ears to your direction. Where I have doubt or discouragement, help me to find conviction and encouragement to live as you desire me to live. I ask that you fill me with your peace on these matters. I ask all this in the power of the Most Holy and Sacred Name of Our Lord, Jesus Christ. Amen.

## *What's Next?*

Now that we've discussed what the laws and precepts of the Church do to help us live in love, let's talk about the Mass and it's role in helping us with that same goal.

# CHAPTER 19. CELEBRATING THE MASS: ENTERING HEAVEN ON EARTH

## *The Mass: A Heavenly Hour*

At every Mass, all throughout the world, no matter what country it takes place in or the language spoken, the same things are happening. The faithful believers in Christ are gathering together to celebrate the reign of love.

### Heaven on Earth

Whenever Mass is celebrated, we get to enter Heaven for an hour. Here, Christ is King, love reigns supreme, and everyone present is united in the joyful celebration of love's eternal victory over sin and death. For one hour, there is no discord and no disagreement. We can put aside our differences and find true peace.

### One Sacrifice Made Present for All Time

This isn't a re-sacrificing of Jesus. It's us entering into eternity and being able to stand at the foot of the cross with John and Christ's Mother, Mary, as Jesus sacrifices His life for ours. We get sanctified in His shed blood and washed clean in the water that flows from His side.

### Preparing for the Last Day

This is where we experience what it will be like on that last day, when Jesus comes to separate the sheep from the goats.

We find, in the Mass, every help needed to ensure that we are counted among the sheep and not the goats when that day arrives.

## All Angels and Saints Are Present

Although unseen by our naked eyes, the angels and saints are all present there as Christ gives His life for ours. They gather at every Mass singing praise to the Lord along with us.

Now that we know what we're receiving in the Mass, let's explore the parts of the Mass.

# *The Opening of the Mass: Awaiting and Celebrating Christ's Triumphant Entrance*

We enter into Mass in a state of preparation. We are waiting for Christ's entrance, gathering together, and preparing our hearts to receive Him.

## Examining Our Conscience

Part of the work we do before Mass is to examine our conscience. Is there anything blocking our ability to receive Him with a clean conscience? Is there anything we need to repent of or set right with Him? If so, we know we can't enter the Wedding Feast of the Lamb like that.

We are like souls in Purgatory, who must deny ourselves Christ for a time so we can cleanse ourselves of those blockages of grace and receive Him with a pure heart.

## Engaging in Prayerful Contemplation

If we know our hearts are clean, we move into prayerful contemplation of Christ's sacrifice. We spend time thanking and praising Him for loving us so much that He invites us to join Him today.

## Rejoicing at His Entrance

After a time of gathering, Christ arrives on the scene in the form of the priest, who through a grace of the Holy Spirit acts in the person of Christ (in persona Christi), accompanied by his assistants. We rise and sing a song of rejoicing that He has returned to redeem us.

## Acknowledging Our Sins and Asking for His Mercy

We then spend time acknowledging our sins and asking for His mercy in a song or chant called the Kýrie, eléison which, literally translated, means Lord, Have Mercy. We then join with the angels and saints in singing "Glory to God" during appropriate seasons.

## Praying the Collect

As we prepare to hear the Word of God read to us, the priest leads us in the Collect - a common prayer where we ask God to open our hearts and minds to receive all the grace He desires for us to receive during the rest of the Mass.

Now that we've examined what the opening contains, let's explore what we do during the Liturgy of the Word, the second portion of the Mass.

# *The Liturgy of the Word: Listening and Responding to God's Love Letters to Humanity*

The Liturgy of the Word is the portion of the Mass during which we read from Sacred Scripture. Similar to a Jewish marriage ceremony, called a Ketubah, this can be likened to the reading of the covenant agreement that we've made with Christ when we gave ourselves to Him. This document – Sacred Scripture – spells out the terms we've agreed to when we entered into a Holy Union with Him.

Throughout history, God's been writing love letters to humanity. That's what the Bible is: A story about God's undying love for humanity, the lengths to which He's gone to save us from ourselves, and His invitation to join us in His quest to teach His children how to love as He does.

## The First Reading: From the Old Testament or from Acts

Usually taken from the Old Testament, but from Acts during the season of Easter, we see what God did to reach His people at the very beginning. We hear what actions He took to redeem us and save us, and what the people's responses were to those actions.

## The Responsorial Psalm: Our Response and the Context

## for the First Reading

The people's answer to that first reading is found in the Psalm of the day. We listen and respond in chorus to that Psalm. It summarizes the big takeaway that God wants us to receive from that first reading and helps put it into context for us.

## The Second Reading: Usually from the Letters of the New Testament

In this reading is found a message that will help us connect the dots between the first reading, the message of the responsorial psalm, and the readings of the Gospel.

## The Gospel Acclamation

As we finish the first readings, we sing a short bit of praise to Christ known as the Alleluia as the priest, standing as Christ through the power of the Holy Spirit, steps up to deliver His word to Us.

## The Gospel: Reminding Us of Christ's Life and His Teachings

The priest or deacon reads from the Gospels a passage that reflects on the Work of Christ on our behalf and His teachings.

*"Likewise deacons must be reverent, not double-tongued, not given to much wine, not greedy for money, holding the mystery of the faith with a pure conscience. But let these also first be tested; then let them serve as deacons, being found blameless. Likewise, their wives must be reverent, not slanderers, temperate, faithful in all things. Let deacons be the husbands of one wife, ruling their children and their own houses well. For those who have served well as deacons obtain for themselves a good standing and great boldness in the faith which is in Christ Jesus." – 1 Timothy 3:8-13*

A deacon is a man ordained to be a bishop's assistant and to serve the Church. He can perform baptisms, marriages, and funerals, but he cannot hear confessions, consecrate the bread and wine to become the body and blood of Christ, anoint the sick, confirm people in the Holy Spirit, or ordain new priests.

## The Homily: Helping Us Apply What We've Heard to Everyday Life

After the readings are completed, the Liturgy of the Word ends with a short teaching given by the priest called the homily. The goal of the homily is to help us connect the dots between these readings and how it is meant to be applied so that we might live out the call to love our neighbor more faithfully.

The priest will often provide historical context to help us unpack the meaning of the things we've heard when modern life doesn't lend itself to a clear understanding.

### The Profession of Faith

Here we profess the beliefs we hold in a public way by reciting the Apostle's Creed during most Masses. For special masses, we recite the longer Nicene Creed which was formulated at the Council of Nicea to combat several heresies that arose. This recitation acts as our consent to the terms and conditions of our marriage covenant with Christ.

### The Universal Prayers

At this point in time, we pray as one for our Church, our Congregation, one another, and any specific intentions we hold in our hearts.

## *The Liturgy of the Eucharist: Entering Into a Covenant with Love*

This part of the Mass IS the wedding feast of the Lamb. It is a renewal of our vows, made to Christ during our Baptism and Confirmation, to partner with Him in bringing more love into the world. Everything we do in this portion of the Mass centers around that renewal.

### The Offertory: An Exchange of Gifts

*"Give, and it will be given to you. Good measure, pressed down, shaken together, running over, will be put into your lap. For with the measure you use it will be measured back to you."*
*- Luke 6:38*

Much more than just putting money in the collection plate, this is our opportunity to show by what we are willing to sacrifice how much we value the sacrifice Christ made for us on the cross.

> *"Contribute to the needs of the saints and seek to show hospitality." – Romans 12:13*

While what we offer to Him by what we give to the Church can never equal what He offers us in return, we want to come as close as we can to it.

## Presentation of the Gifts and the Preparation of the Altar

Here the congregation presents their gifts to the priest as he prepares the altar to receive the gifts of love. This mirrors the Old Testament, where the people brought their sacrifices to the temple priests. Now, we have one High priest that we offer our sacrifices to, Jesus Christ. The priest acts in the person of Christ, receiving them on His behalf.

## Prayer over the Offerings and the Eucharistic Prayers

The priest then prays over the offerings and the people. It isn't just the gifts that are being consecrated in this moment. We are also being set apart (the meaning of the word consecration) for Christ as living sacrifices, just as Christ is an eternally living sacrifice made for us.

It is during this consecration that Transubstantiation takes place, when Christ fully enters into the bread and wine, transforming it into His body and His blood even though it retains the appearance, smell, shape, and taste of ordinary bread and wine.

## The Lord's Prayer and the Sign of Peace

> *"Our Father, Who art in heaven, hallowed be Thy name; Thy kingdom come; Thy will be done on earth as it is in heaven. Give us this day our daily bread; and forgive us our trespasses as we forgive those who trespass against us; and lead us not into temptation, but deliver us from evil." – Matthew 6:9-13*

All those gathered recite the Lord's prayer at this time, reminding ourselves of the call to forgive and the importance of allowing love to reign over our lives. We then exchange signs of peace with one another as proof of our having forgiven one another and a sign of our readiness for the gift that is to come.

## The Lamb of God

We sing or recite the Lamb of God, acknowledging Christ's

presence in the Eucharist.

Lamb of God, you take away the sins of the world,

have mercy on us.

Lamb of God, you take away the sins of the world,

have mercy on us.

Lamb of God, you take away the sins of the world,

grant us peace.

The first part is taken from John 1:29:

*"Next day, John saw Jesus coming towards him; and he said, Look, this is the Lamb of God; look, this is he who takes away the sin of the world. "*

Followed by a specific request for His mercy on us and, finally, peace in Him.

## Communion: Reception of the Eucharist

Every Mass offers the Eucharist. It wouldn't be a Mass without it, just as you couldn't have a proper Jewish wedding ceremony without a wedding feast.

All those who are prepared to receive Christ do so while we sing songs of love to Christ, acknowledging the incredible gift of being able to enter into this union with Him. Communion is the ultimate consummation of our vows to Christ, entering into a total union of love with the ultimate source of all love.

It is important that we not receive communion when we know we've done something to hurt Him but haven't confessed that yet. We don't want to betray Jesus with a kiss, as Judas did, or to take this gift for granted.

## Prayer after Communion and Final Blessings

After communion, now filled with Christ's love, the priest offers us a final blessing in preparation for us being sent back out into the world as "Christ bearers," carrying His message of love to a world dying for lack of it.

Now that we know what's happening at the Mass, let's engage in some exercises to help us better understand this incredible gift of the Mass.

## *Exercises*

Journal your answers to the following questions:

1. What did I think the Mass was before this lesson?
2. How does this lesson impact how I see the Mass now?
3. What will I do differently based on this new understanding?

## *Let's Pray*

Heavenly Father, I thank you and praise you and bless you for the love you shower me with each day. Help me not to take the Mass for granted. Help me to prepare myself to receive you with a heart filled with joy at the wonder of your love and the pains you take to enter into a perfect, spousal union with me. Help me to open myself up to receive all the love that you desire to pour into me so that I may share that abundance with others. I ask all this in the power of the Most Holy and Sacred Name of the Lord Jesus Christ. Amen.

## *What's Next?*

Now that we've talked about the Mass and how it helps us unite ourselves to Christ's divine love so we can give that love to others, let's talk about Christ's mother, Mary, and her role in helping us live lives of authentic love.

z

# CHAPTER 20. MARY: A PERFECT MODEL OF LIVING FOR THE SAKE OF LOVE

## *Her Sinless Perfection: The Father's Gift to His Son*

When the Angel Gabriel greeted Mary, He didn't call her by name. He called her by a peculiar title: "Kecharitomene," (κεχαριτωμένη) in the Greek.

"καὶ εἰσελθὼν πρὸς αὐτὴν εἶπεν: χαῖρε, κεχαριτωμένη, ὁ κύριος μετὰ σοῦ." - Luke 1:28

That word is used one and only one time in all of recorded history for one and only one person. Although in English this is often translated as simply "full of grace," or (weaker), "favored one," the Greek meaning of it is far richer and deeper.

The ke that comes before charito is a perfect passive participle, indicating that the charitoo (bestowing of grace) action is something given in the past, carried into the present, and continuing on into the future.

The -mene ending tells us this action is not something the person did for themselves. It was bestowed upon them by a divine action.

Thus, a more accurate translation than full of grace would be to translate that passage as "Hail to the one who is, was, and always will be filled with the grace of the Holy Spirit." But that would be quite a mouthful.

Scripture tells us that all those who sin are slaves to sin.

*"And Jesus answered them, Believe me when I tell you this; everyone who acts sinfully is the slave of sin," - John 8:34*

St. Paul tells us that we who are baptized are not born of a woman enslaved, but of a freeborn woman because we are baptized into Christ whose mother was sinless.

*"Therefore, brothers, we are not children of the slave woman, but of the free woman." - Galatians 4:31*

God's restoration of Mary to a sinless state was His gift to His son and took place at the moment of her conception. Jesus deserved a perfect mother and got one! That perfection didn't come as a result of anything she did.

It was a gift given to her for a singular and specific task she alone could carry out: being the mother of God (since Jesus is God.) She still received salvation through Jesus Christ...it is simply that her salvation came at the moment of her conception and not after a fall from grace.

Simply put, she was given special help to ensure that her heart never got wounded by either her own sins or the sins of others so that she could give and receive the love of God without fail and teach her son and all of us how to give and receive love without fail, too.

Now that you have a better understanding of what Catholics believe about Mary and her sinless perfection, let's talk about how her perfect obedience to God in every challenging moment models for us how to live out the call to love when we are most challenged.

## *Her Perfect Obedience: Modeling Trust in the Lord*

Mary's obedience to God was perfect. From beginning to end, she did everything God asked of her without hesitation.

When called to marry Joseph rather than live a life for God, she submitted to God's will.

At the Annunciation, she gave up her will and her own plans for her life to follow God's will and His plan for her life despite knowing the risks she faced of being accused of adultery or fornication.

At Christ's birth, she gave up her will and allowed her child to be born in a stable. When Joseph told her they were to go to Egypt, she gave up her will and left without complaint.

Joseph died sometime after he was found in the Temple at age 12 and before Jesus's public ministry began at the age of 30. We know this because he is never mentioned after that point in the Gospels and, at Jesus's death, Jesus gave her over to John's care. If she were married, her care would have been Joseph's legal responsibility. Mary served her husband faithfully throughout the entirety of their marriage.

When Jesus began his public ministry, she gave up everything to follow Him and help Him with His mission.

When Jesus gave His life on the Cross, she surrendered her will and her desires for her son's life to accept God's will and God's plans without complaint.

When Jesus said, "Woman, behold your son!" she accepted her new assignment to care for His beloved disciples.

She did this all without complaint, trusting always in the Lord's will and the Lord's ways even when she didn't understand why it was necessary to do what she was doing.

In that obedience, she models for us how we should live: always ready to surrender our will to the Lord's. Always trusting in His will and His way, even when it seems to go against our own desires.

Now that we understand the role that Mary plays in helping us to act like she did, let's talk about how Mary's perfect faithfulness, obedience, and charity become a model our own lives as followers of Christ.

## *Her Eternal Virginity: Modeling Faithful Love*

Mary kept herself set apart for love her entire life. She dedicated every action, every word spoken, and every part of her being to Him.

She practiced perfect modesty, ensuring that only the God who is love ever saw her full glory. She remained faithful in her body, mind, heart, and soul so that she could give all of her time, energy, and attention to Jesus, who is Love Incarnate, and those who served Him.

In the life she lived, she modeled the way that those who follow Christ are called to dedicate everything they have and are to His service without holding anything back of themselves or their gifts.

Now that we understand how her perpetual virginity models what faithful love looks like, mark this lesson complete. Let's examine how Mary modeled perfection in the way she loved those around her.

## *Her Actions: Modeling Perfect Charity*

*"In the days that followed, Mary rose up and went with all haste to a town of Juda, in the hill country where Zachary dwelt; and there entering in she gave Elizabeth greeting." - Luke 1:39-40*

Mary braved a 70-mile journey from Nazareth to the hill country of Juda while in the first stages of pregnancy in order to tend to her elderly cousin, Elizabeth, who was pregnant with John the Baptist. She put her own needs and desires aside to focus on serving the needs of others, modeling perfect Christian charity for us.

*"Here the supply of wine failed; whereupon Jesus' mother said to him, They have no wine left." - John 2:3*

It was Mary who noticed the distress of the servants at the wedding feast of Cana, uncovered the young couple's need, and - moved with pity for them - interceded on their behalf. She took their needs straight to Christ, modeling how we ourselves are to behave.

She didn't wait for God to ask her to serve others. She took it on herself to be on the lookout for opportunities to serve others and then brought those things to Christ's attention.

*And Jesus, seeing his mother there, and the disciple, too, whom he loved, standing by, said to his mother, Woman, this is thy son. - John 19:26*

In this passage, we see proof of Mary being a widow. When a man's mother became a widow through the death of his father, Jewish law required that he take care of her. This is why Jesus brought Mary with her everywhere He went.

Had Jesus any biological brothers, the task of caring for Mary would have fallen to them in the absence of His father. However, we see this is not the case. Thus, at His death, He made sure there was someone to provide for her in his place, the beloved disciple. He treats this disciple as a brother by bestowing the responsibility for her care on him.

When asked to adopt Christ's beloved disciple as her own (and all of us who are faithful in following Him are HIs beloved disciple), she accepted the charge without complaint. Even those who betrayed him, like Peter, and those who deserted or abandoned him she chose to love as her own, remaining with them in the Upper Room where they celebrated the Last Supper with Christ all the way through Pentecost.

Pentecost is that day when the tongues of flame settled over everyone gathered in that room and they stepped out in faith, on fire with the Holy Spirit, to convert 3,000 people.

This was an incredibly hard thing to ask of a grieving mother - to adopt as her own children those who failed to be faithful and loyal to her son - but she accepted this, forgave them as Christ did, and chose to pour the love for Christ she held in her heart into their lives. This models for us how we are to behave toward those who fail us and those who fail the ones we love most: Love them anyway and pour the love of Christ that lives in our hearts into them.

*"Never be afraid of loving the Blessed Virgin too much. You can never love her more than Jesus did." - St. Maximilian Kolbe*

Having seen what Mary's Perfect Charity does to help us live lives of authentic love, it's time for our exercises.

## *Exercises*

Journal your answers to the following questions:

1. How did I feel about Mary before this lesson?
2. How do I feel about her now?
3. Do I plan to use Mary as a model for my life?
4. If not, why not?
5. If you already do, what benefits have you experienced from doing so?
6. If not, do you plan to change that?
7. What do you think Jesus would say about that?

## *Let's Pray*

Lord Jesus Christ, you gave us your perfect mother to be our own at the foot of the cross. We thank you for the gift of a model of perfect motherhood and womanhood. We thank you for her perfect example of Christian living that we might follow that example. Please help us to grow in our appreciation of our Blessed Mother and to share this appreciation with others. We ask all this in the power of your most Holy and Sacred Name. Amen.

## *What's Next?*

We've talked about Mary and her role in helping us live lives of authentic love, let's talk about the Saints and what they do to help us.

z

# CHAPTER 21. THE SAINTS: A GREAT CLOUD OF WITNESSES

## *The Saints: Ordinary People Living Extraordinary Lives of Love*

"Why then, since we are watched from above by such a cloud of witnesses, let us rid ourselves of all that weighs us down, of the sinful habit that clings so closely, and run, with all endurance, the race for which we are entered."- Hebrews 12:11

Unlike Mary, who received Christ's salvation at the moment of her conception, the Saints are ordinary individuals like you and I. The Church elevates them because they show what is possible for ordinary people to do when they dedicate their lives to spreading the message of love.

Many of them wrestled with the call to love. It's not easy to choose love over selfishness. Their lives provide us encouragement to believe that if they can do it, we can, too. Their struggles provide us hope that we can, like them, conquer our temptations and rid ourselves of our vices.

*The scene of your approach now is mount Sion, is the heavenly Jerusalem, city of the living God; here are gathered thousands upon thousands of angels, here is the assembly of those first-born sons whose names are written in heaven, here is God sitting in judgement on all men, here are the spirits of just men, now made perfect; here is Jesus, the spokesman of the new covenant, and the sprinkling of his blood, which has better things to say than Abel's had. – Hebrews 12:22-24*

The lessons they learned and the legacy they left behind provide us guidance in how to choose love when it's hardest and most difficult to do so, as well as a constant reminder of what is to be gained when we do.

Now that we see what the Saints provide for us and why the Church elevates them, mark this lesson complete. Let's discuss how we can be confident that praying to them is not rejecting the laws of love or failing to follow Christ.

## *The Saints: Eternally United to Christ*

In Baptism, everyone who believes in Christ becomes a member of His body.

*We too, all of us, have been baptized into a single body by the power of a single Spirit, Jews and Greeks, slaves and free men alike; we have all been given drink at a single source, the one Spirit. - 1 Cor 12:13*

All those who die in Christ live in Him.

*And if we have died with Christ, we have faith to believe that we shall share his life. - Romans 6:8*

Their bodies die, but their souls remain in Him until the Last Judgment, when a glorified body is provided to them and their body and soul are reunited.

As Christ Himself stated, God

*"...is not the God of the dead, but the God of the living. You are therefore greatly mistaken." - Mark 12:27*

Put simply: Everything dies, but love remains untouched by time. Therefore, we can feel confident in our ability to call on the saints and ask for their help.

We, in fact, see them offering prayers in Revelation 8:3-4:

*"There was another angel that came and took his stand at the altar, with a censer of gold; and incense was given him in plenty, so that he could make an offering on the golden altar*

*before the throne, out of the prayers said by all the saints. So, from the angel's hand, the smoke of the incense went up in God's presence, kindled by the saints' prayer."*

Prayer is not worship. Worship requires sacrifice. Prayer is a petition or request. We can request prayers from any living person, and that includes the saints. However, we are to worship no one but God.

For those who are concerned about the prohibitions against speaking to the dead found in Scriptures, such as this:

*Now if people say to you, "Consult the ghosts and the familiar spirits that chirp and mutter; should not a people consult their gods, the dead on behalf of the living, for teaching and for instruction?" Surely, those who speak like this will have no dawn! - Isaiah 8:9-10*

First, we do not consult the saints. We offer our prayers to God through them and seek their intercession on our behalf.

Why not go straight to Jesus? Because the saints know Jesus far better than we do and know how to approach Him in ways that will incline Him to favor our requests.

Scripture does teach us as believers to:

*"...pray for one another..." assuring us that "...the prayer of the righteous person has great power." – James 5:16*

Who could be more righteous than those who are already in Heaven?

Second, know that the Church does not easily name someone a saint. While the process of declaring someone a saint, known as canonization, is not mentioned in Scripture it is because the process came to be after Scripture was formalized.

The Church received the authority to do this through Christ's, who said:

*" I promise you, all that you bind on earth shall be bound in heaven, and all that you loose on earth shall be loosed in heaven." – Matthew 18:18*

With that authority came the authority to determine the

process used by which we should bind and loose. The process of sainthood begins with a thorough examination of their life for proof of holiness. This process can't even be started until a minimum of five years after their death.

Furthermore, there must be at least two miracles attributed to their intercession that are definitively not explainable by science. If the Church declares someone a saint, you may be confident they are safe to call upon.

Also, we are not seeking for the saints to tell us our futures or to teach us and instruct us. We are seeking their help and support in lifting our prayers to God, but we are ultimately leaving the outcome in God's hands. No saint is going to go against the will of God, or they wouldn't be a saint.

Now that we know why calling upon the saints does not violate the prohibitions against speaking to the dead, mark this lesson complete. In our next lesson, we'll explore the saints as portraits of courage.

## *The Saints: Portraits of Courage*

The saints didn't just live their lives for love. Quite often, they lost their lives because of their devotion to Christ and their faithfulness to spreading His message of love to those in need of it.

These deaths were often gruesome and tortuous. St. Peter was crucified upside down by his own request because he didn't feel worthy to be crucified in the same manner as Christ. That's why there's an upside-down cross behind the Chair of St. Peter in the Vatican.

St. Stephen was stoned to death in Acts. So was St. Paul. St. Lucy's eyes were plucked out by those who wanted her to renounce Christ. St. Lawrence was roasted alive and quipped to his torturers, "I'm done on this side. You may turn me over now."

These brave men and women give us examples of courage to follow and hope that we, too, can be faithful through to the end.

Having explored the portraits of courage that the saints

provide to us, mark this lesson complete.

## *Patron Saints: Personal Champions*

In the Catholic faith, our parents are encouraged to give us a name with at least one Catholic saint in it. That saint is to be our personal champion, helping us in our battle to reach Heaven. This saint is asked to look over and watch out for us throughout our lives.

When we grow older, we are encouraged to choose a patron saint for ourselves when we prepare for confirmation. If you are coming into the Church as an adult, you will also be encouraged to choose a patron saint for yourself.

Let's start our exercises.

## *Exercises*

Journal your answer to the following questions:

1. What did I believe about the saints before this lesson?

2. What do I believe about them now?

3. How will that change how I live out my faith?

4. Do I have a patron saint?

5. If so, do I know who they are?

6. If not, pray and ask God to assign you one.

## *Let's Pray*

Holy Spirit, we know that Christ sent you to guide us in all things. Help us to deepen our appreciation of the saints and to treat them as friends in the faith. Please guide me to my patron saint if I do not yet know him or her. Help me to learn to walk and talk with them so they can help me win the battle for love each day. We ask all this in the power of the most Holy and Sacred Name of our Lord and Savior, Jesus Christ. Amen.

## *What's Next?*

Now that we've got a better understanding of what role the saints play in helping us to live out lives of love, let's explore the Rosary and what it offers us.

z

# CHAPTER 22. THE ROSARY: TEACHING US HOW TO CHOOSE LOVE IN EVERY CIRCUMSTANCE

The Rosary is a method of meditating and praying over Scripture. It is not mentioned in Scripture because it was introduced into the Church after Scripture was compiled.

The Hail Mary is almost entirely Scriptural. Most of the entire final petition was published by St. Peter Canisius in his 1555 Catechism and eleven years later, the Council of Trent finalized the prayer and added its conclusion, "now and at the hour of our death. Amen." It was given official Vatican approval in 1568.

## *History of the Rosary*

It began as a means of praying the Psalms. 150 beads kept track of the 150 Psalms. Later, the Jesus Prayer (Lord Jesus Christ, son of God, have mercy on me) was added. The Our Father, known as the Paternoster in Latin, was also prayed 150 times.

In 1214, the Church was under attack by Albigensian heretics teaching that only the spirit is good and all material things, the body included, are bad. Therefore, the body was evil and people were imprisoned in their evil body. The only way to experience salvation was to free themselves from their evil body. Many souls were confused and being lost to this teaching.

St. Dominic prayed for the grace to be able to turn the tide in the Church's favor and convert those who didn't believe. He ad a tremendous devotion to Mary and she appeared to him, presenting him with the rosary and the beads, along with the prayers to say.

The result? St. Dominic began to win the victory, converting souls and draining the Albigensian sect of its membership.

It's broken into 4 Sections, which reflect on the mystery (a truth so profound that we must spend an eternity unpacking the full meaning of it) of a God who loves us so much He is willing to take on our sins and die for us to save us.

The four mysteries are:

1. The Joyful Mysteries: The life of Christ from conception through age 12

2. The Sorrowful Mysteries: The passion of Christ from the agony through the crucifixion

3. The Luminous Mysteries: Meditations on the ministry of Christ

4. The Glorious Mysteries: The resurrection through the first fulfillment of Christ's promises

Each section provides support and guidance for a different stage of love:

The Joyful Mysteries: Saying "yes" to love when it's easier to say "no."

The Sorrowful Mysteries: Choosing to love when it's hardest to love.

The Luminous Mysteries: Reminders of the importance of staying filled up with God's love in the Sacraments

The Glorious Mysteries: Reminders of the great things waiting for us ahead when we choose to love like Christ.

> *"If you wish to convert anyone to the fullness of the knowledge of Our Lord and of His Mystical Body, then teach him the Rosary. One of two things will happen. Either he will stop saying the Rosary — or he will get the gift of faith." - Archbishop Fulton Sheen*

Now that we've examined what the Rosary offers us in helping us to understand how to live out our call to love, mark this lesson complete. Let's take a closer look at the Joyful Mysteries.

## *The Joyful Mysteries: Encouraging Us to Say Yes to Love*

Saying "yes" to God often requires a leap of faith and a departure from our own plans. The Joyful Mysteries help us to keep saying yes when things get hard.

### The Annunciation (Luke 1:26-38)

As we meditate on the moment that Mary put aside her plans to say "Yes" to God's plans for her life, we ask for the grace to say "Yes" to carrying God's love to others in accordance with His plan even when it interrupts our own.

### The Visitation (Luke 1:39-56)

While meditating on the difficult, dangerous journey that Mary undertook to bring the message of Christ to Elizabeth, we ask for the grace to be willing to go the distance and brave the dangers required to carry God's love to others and show up ready to serve, rather than be served, as she did.

### The Nativity (Luke 2:4-20)

Focusing our minds on the moment when pure, unconditional love chose to enter the world in the middle of the messiness and stench of a stable and then shine a light so bright over the top of that stable that all those who were wandering in darkness might find their way to Him by it and those who were seeking wisdom might find that light and, through it, find Him.

In this meditation we ask for the courage to open up about the messiness and stench of our past so that through our story, the glory of God's love may be revealed. We also ask that He then shine a light so bright over the top of that story that those who feel hopeless about their own pasts and wander in darkness because of it may be filled with hope and those seeking wisdom may find that wisdom in our story and be inspired to seek God's love because of it.

### The Presentation in the Temple (Luke 2:21-39)

Examining this mystery, we find encouragement to follow Christ and Mary in their example, presenting themselves before Church authority in obedience to the Law despite the risks involved in doing so. We ask for that same courage to obey the Church's divinely inspired teachings so that we, like Mary and Christ, might receive their blessing.

### The Finding in the Temple (Luke 2:42-51)

Reflecting on this time when Joseph and Mary lost sight of the child Jesus for three days, we are encouraged to keep watch over our lives. The minute we notice we've lost sight of love, and aren't making it the priority it needs to be, to find the courage to turn our lives around and pursue love with everything we've got.

Now that we know what the Joyful Mysteries do to encourage us on our journey of love, let's explore the role the Sorrowful Mysteries of the Rosary play in helping us continue choosing love when it's most challenging.

## *The Sorrowful Mysteries: Choosing Love When Its Most Challenging*

Love doesn't always feel good. It doesn't always bring the rewards or gratitude we expect it should. Sometimes, it brings us agony, pain, punishment, injustice, rejection, and even death. While meditating on the Sorrowful Mysteries, we ask Christ for the graces needed to choose the most loving action to take in the face of humanity's worst.

### The Agony in the Garden (Matthew 26:36-46)

While meditating on this mystery, we ask for the graces needed to move past how we feel in the moment to choose what is most loving. This is especially challenging to do when we know our sacrifice won't be valued or appreciated by those we are sacrificing everything to save. Our willingness to make that sacrifice is critical to our growth in our capacity to give and receive love.

### The Scourging at the Pillar (Matthew 27:26)

Reflecting on this mystery helps us to bear the wrongs done to us with the same patience with which Christ bore our wrongdoing against Him. We are reminded that people who are starving for love are like blind beggars who enter a buffet full of food.

They become frustrated by the smells and can hear people eating all around them but don't know how to get their needs met, so they end up whacking people with their cane, smashing plates, and knocking over food in their desperation to get their needs met. They don't mean to hurt anyone or to ruin things, they simply don't know how else to get the help they need.

### The Crowning with Thorns (Matthew 27:27-30)

As we meditate on this mystery, we reflect on all the ridicule, scorn, abuse, humiliations, and degradation that Christ suffered so that He could lead us to love. We ask Him for the grace to see the lovable people behind their unlovable behaviors so we can continue showing them love even when they mistreat, abuse, abandon, humiliate, and degrade us. We don't want to let their behavior change who we are or follow their lead.

### The Carrying of the Cross (Matthew 27:31-32)

During this Mystery, we reflect on the heavy burdens caused by our own failures to love that Christ carries for us. We ask for the graces needed to carry burdens imposed on us when other people fail to love without grumbling or complaining, but to carry it with steadfast joy knowing that this cross we carry now is a sign of how much we love the Lord. How we carry that little sliver of a cross He asks us to carry for His sake shows Him how much we appreciate His willingness to carry the tremendous weight of His cross for us.

### The Crucifixion of Christ (Matthew 27:34-35)

Putting our egos and our own will to death so that Christ's will that we should love one another may be done instead is one of the most challenging and painful things we can do. It can feel like we are dying - because part of us is - but we cannot enter the glory and resurrection phase that comes on the other side of a relationship conflict without going through the cross and crucifixion phase. We seek Christ's help in staying on that cross all the way through to what feels like "the end."

Now that we understand more about how the sorrowful mysteries help us choose love when it seems easier to just give up and walk away, let's explore the encouragement to continue choosing love that is found in the Glorious Mysteries.

## *The Glorious Mysteries: Encouraging Us to Continue Living for Love*

We reflect on the Glorious Mysteries to remind ourselves of Love's faithfulness, of His promises that what we sacrifice in the Joyful and Sorrowful moments of life will not go unrewarded. We are, in these Mysteries, reminded that every Cross and Crucifixion moment in a relationship heralds the coming of a Glory and Resurrection moment. This helps us find the courage to continue living lives for the sake of love.

### The Resurrection (John 20:1-20)

In the Mystery of the Resurrection, we bring to Christ all the relationships in our life that we destroyed with our selfish behaviors along with the relationships that died due to the pain that other people's selfishness caused us and ask Him to breathe new life into them.

### The Ascension (Mark 16:19)

Reflecting on Christ's ascension, we are reminded that the world and its allures are not lasting. The only thing worth living for and sacrificing everything to gain is love, for with it comes all good things. We ask for Christ's help in rejecting the temporary distractions of the world so we can live for love alone.

### Descent of the Holy Spirit (Acts 2:1-4)

While meditating on the moment the Holy Spirit filled the Upper Room and all those gathered into it with Christ's unconditional, eternal love, we are encouraged to reach out to

Him and ask for the Holy Spirit to fill us with that same love. We want to be set on fire with a passionate, all-consuming love that burns away the selfish desires which act as obstacles to filling our lives with love.

### The Assumption of the Blessed Virgin (John 8:51)

An ancient tradition recorded in the ProtoEvangelium of James states that Christ took the Blessed Virgin, after she fell into a deep sleep, into Heaven without allowing her body to suffer any hint of decay. When we meditate on this mystery, we are reminded that death can't touch us if we unite ourselves completely to Christ and allow Him to fill us with His love.

### The Coronation of the Virgin Mary (Revelation 12;1)

*"When the chief Shepherd appears, you will receive the unfading crown of glory"* - 1 Peter 5:4

In this mystery, when we meditate on Mary receiving a crown of glory from her son in reward for her faithful service to Him, we are encouraged to remember that love is the only crown any person truly needs. It is the ultimate crown of glory to be known for the love we share with others. We seek the Holy Spirit's help to conquer selfishness and choose to allow love to reign supreme in our hearts.

## *The Luminous Mysteries: Deepening Our Appreciation of the Sacraments*

The Luminous Mysteries serve as reminders of the importance of keeping ourselves filled up with love by engaging the sacraments as often as we are able.

### The Baptism and Confirmation of Christ (Mark 1:9-11)

As we meditate on the moment when Christ received His baptism and the confirmation of His status as the Son of God, received by the Holy Spirit, we are reminded of the role they play in helping us live lives of authentic love.

In Baptism, we invite God's love to take up residence in our heart and to remove from us whatever blocks the path to love. In Confirmation, we promise to enter the fight to make sure that everyone has an opportunity to experience the joy that comes from unconditional love. As we meditate on this mystery, we ask that Christ help us to renew the vows we made to Him (or to make them in the first place if we haven't yet done so) and live His love ever more faithfully.

## The Wedding Feast at Cana (John 2:1-11)

In this Luminous Mystery, we see the role that Christ plays in restoring joy (the wine was a symbol for the joy that living for God brings) into our lives. When we bring our emptiness to Him, and "do whatever He tells us to do," He will restore the joy in our lives and our relationships. This is a good meditation not only for those who are feeling dryness in their marriage or their vocation, but for anyone called to service others.

## Preaching of the Good News & Call to Repentance (Matthew 4:17)

This Mystery focuses on Christ's public ministry and His message that we are all called to experience the beauty of unconditional love, but to do so we must first turn away from selfishness. We must seek His help in the confessional to restore the strength required to choose love when we recognize we've failed in our quest to love as Christ loves so that we can heal our hearts and restore our capacity to hold onto love.

## The Transfiguration (Matthew 17:1-13)

In meditating on Christ's Transfiguration moment, where the pure glory of love was revealed to Peter, James, and John, we are encouraged to allow Christ to transfigure our lives, too. We want everyone we meet to experience the radiant, pure love of Christ with every encounter. This is what is possible when we live a sacramental life dedicated to love.

## The Institution of the Eucharist (Mark 14:22-26)]

Meditating on the moment when Christ instituted the Eucharist at His last supper, we grow in our appreciation for the priests who make the Eucharist present for us so that it is possible for us to become living tabernacles as Christ makes His home in our hearts.

Now that we can see a bit more of how the Luminous Mysteries help us to grow in our appreciation for the Sacraments, mark this lesson complete. Let's engage in some exercises to help us deepen our understanding.

## *Exercises*

Journal your answers to the following questions:

1. Do you pray the Rosary?

2. If not, why not?

3. Will you begin praying it now?

4. Which set of Mysteries speaks most to your life today?

5. If you do pray the Rosary already, what do you love most about it?

## *Let's Pray*

Holy Spirit, giver of all good things, you bring God's blessings to those who ask for them. You delivered the Rosary through the hands of our Blessed Mother, Mary. Please help us to grow in our appreciation of this gift and to incorporate it into our daily lives so that we may grow ever closer to Christ. We ask all this in the power of the most Holy and Sacred Name of our Lord and Savior, Jesus Christ. Amen.

## *What's Next?*

Now that we've learned how the Rosary works to help support us in our quest to live lives of authentic love, let's explore the prayers of the Rosary and what they teach us about love.

z

# CHAPTER 23. THE PRAYERS OF THE ROSARY

Remember: Prayer and worship are not the same thing. Prayer is a humble petition and a request for help. We petition Mary and the Saints for help. We worship God alone.

### Opening Prayers:
1. The Sign of the Cross
2. The Apostle's Creed
3. The Our Father
4. The Hail Mary (3x)
5. A Glory Be
6. O My Jesus

### For Each Decade:
1. The Our Father
2. The Hail Mary (10x)
3. A Glory Be
4. O My Jesus

### After the Rosary:
1. Hail, Holy Queen
2. Concluding Rosary Prayer

Now that you know what prayers are to be said, and in

what order we say them, let's talk about how to say them and why we say them.

## *The Sign of the Cross*

### What We Say

In the name of the Father (touch your forehead), and of the Son (touch the center of your chest), and of the Holy (touch your left shoulder) Spirit (touch your right shoulder). Amen.

### Why We Say That

By marking ourselves with the cross, we remind ourselves that we who are baptized belong to God who is love itself. He purchased our lives with His cross and we bear that mark out of our gratitude for what He has done for us. Everything we do is meant to be done in Christ, with Christ, and through Christ so that we are always operating in alignment with God and taking direction from the Holy Spirit. With our words, we acknowledge our belief in the Holy Trinity, the Father of love, the Son who is love's Undying hope, and the Holy Spirit who brings us all joy.

Now that you understand why we, as Catholics, make the sign of the cross, let's discuss the Apostle's Creed.

## *The Apostle's Creed*

### What We Say

I believe in God, the Father almighty, Creator of heaven and earth, and in Jesus Christ, His only Son, our Lord, who was conceived by the Holy Spirit, born of the Virgin Mary, suffered under Pontius Pilate, was crucified, died and was buried; He descended into hell; on the third day He rose again from the dead; He ascended into heaven, and is seated at the right hand of God the Father almighty; from there He will come to judge the living and the dead.

I believe in the Holy Spirit, the Holy Catholic Church, the communion of saints, the forgiveness of sins, the resurrection of the body, and life everlasting. Amen.

### Why We Say It

As mentioned earlier, this simple prayer is a concise summary of the main points of belief common to all Catholics.

### How We Say It

When praying the Rosary, we recite this prayer while holding the crucifix as a reminder of all that we believe.

## *The Our Father*

### What We Say

Our Father, who art in Heaven, hallowed be thy name. Thy kingdom come, thy will be done, on earth as it is in Heaven.

Give us this day our daily bread, and forgive us our trespasses as we forgive those who trespass against us. And lead us not into temptation but deliver us from evil. Amen

### Why We Say It

We follow the example of prayer that Jesus gave to us in Matthew 6:9-13 as we ask for His help in loving our neighbor as ourselves and forgiving all trespasses as He has forgiven all of ours so that we may one day experience the joy that comes when love reigns supreme in our hearts.

### How We Say It

The Our Father is recited on the first bead after the Crucifix and on the first bead before each decade of Hail Mary's.

## *The Hail Mary*

### What We Pray

Hail Mary, full of grace, the Lord is with you. (Luke 1:28)

Blessed are you among women, and blessed is the fruit of your womb, Jesus (Luke 1:42)

Holy Mary (holy means set apart for God), Mother of God (Luke 1:43), pray for us sinners now and at the hour of death.

Amen.

### Why We Pray It

This beautiful prayer is a reflection on the great gift of the

Incarnation of Christ. This prayer begins with Scripture and ends with a request for Mary to pray for us now and at the hour of our death, when the battle for love will be toughest and the stakes highest. After all, we don't want to lose the gift of Salvation by rejecting it at the last moment.

### How We Pray It

We recite this prayer and ask for the grace of an increase in faith on the first bead after the Our Father, an increase in hope on the bead after that, and an increase in charity on the final bead before the recitation of the Mysteries begins. Then, we recite it ten times after each Our Father (that's why they are called a decade), asking for Mary's help to grow in our understanding of that mystery and how we are to live out its particular call to love.

Now that we understand the value of the Hail Mary, let's talk about the Glory Be.

## *The Glory Be*

### What We Pray

Glory be to the Father, and to the Son, and to the Holy Spirit. As it was in the beginning, is now, and ever shall be. World without end. Amen.

### Why We Pray It

This prayer is four short lines. One line of gratitude for love, for love's promise that we can be better tomorrow than who we are today, and for love's gift of hope that keeps us moving in the right direction. One line that acknowledges that love never dies. One line that promises an eternal home for those who persevere. One word that says we believe in the promise.

### How We Pray It

This prayer is said after the last "Hail Mary" in each decade.

Now that we know what we say and why we say the Glory Be, let's talk about the "Oh, My Jesus" prayer.

## *Oh, My Jesus*

### What We Say

Oh, My Jesus. Forgive us our sins. Save us from the fires of Hell. Lead all souls to Heaven, especially those in most need of thy mercy. Amen.

### Why We Say it

This simple prayer requests divine forgiveness of our own failures to love along with the salvation of our own soul and the souls of everyone else.

### How We Say It

Recited after the Glory Be.

Now that we see what the Glory Be contains, mark this lesson complete. Let's examine the Hail, Holy Queen.

## *Hail, Holy Queen*

### What We Pray

Hail, Holy Queen, Mother of Mercy. Our Life, our sweetness, and our hope. To thee do we cry, poor banished children of Eve. To thee do we send up our sighs, mourning, and weeping in this Valley of Tears. Turn then, Oh Most Gracious Advocate, thine eyes of mercy toward us and after this our exile, show unto us the Blessed Fruit of Thy womb, Jesus, Oh Clement, Oh Loving, Oh sweet Virgin Mary. Pray for us, Oh Holy Mother of God that we may be made worthy of the promises of Christ. Amen.

### Why We Pray It

This longer prayer asks the Mother of Christ to come to our aid during especially difficult moments, and to help us to see the face of Jesus when our time for eternity arrives.

### How We Pray It

Recited at the end of the five decades.

## *Concluding Prayer*

(Verse) Let us pray,

(Response) O God, whose only begotten Son, by His life, death, and resurrection, has purchased for us the rewards of eternal salvation. Grant, we beseech Thee, that while meditating on these mysteries of the most holy Rosary of the Blessed Virgin Mary, that we may both imitate what they contain and obtain what they promise, through Christ our Lord. Amen.

### Why We Pray It

We begin this prayer by acknowledging once again the precious gift of salvation that Jesus purchased for us in His crucifixion. We ask also that Mary come and help us become more like her son, shaping and forming us the way she did with Him into a picture of perfect love.

If you're wondering why we can't just ask Jesus directly, we can. But Mary teaches us the right way to approach Jesus, since she knows His heart better than anyone, so that we're going to get our requests answered faster, with less effort and energy required, than we could on our own.

### When We Pray It

This is the final prayer of the Rosary.

## *A Reminder About the Nature of Prayer*

Spells demand things of God. They arrogantly assume that our way is the best way and that what we want is what is best for us and everyone else. They expect God to bend to our will, rather than asking for His help bending our will to His.

When you pray, you are entering into a conversation with God about your desires and needs. You are bending your will to God's.

You are acknowledging that He is infinitely wiser, more knowledgeable, and possesses far greater understanding not only of your own circumstances and needs but of all those around you. He sees the entire picture, while you see a mere fragment of that image. We, therefore, know that we may request something but God alone can determine whether and how it is best to fulfill that request.

We do not know that our prayer is answered when we get what we want the way we asked to receive it. We know that our prayer is being answered when our hearts, and our thoughts, begin to change. We know our prayers are being answered when we grow in love, joy, hope, peace, patience, kindness, generosity, and all of the virtues required for love to flourish and thrive. Let's work on our Exercises.

## *Exercises*

Journal your answers to the following questions:

1. Were you familiar with the prayers of the Rosary before this chapter?

2. If so, what did you think of them before reading this chapter?

3. What do you think of the prayers now?

4. Do you feel encouraged to pray them?

5. Do you find yourself hesitant to pray any of them?

6. If so, which one(s) and why?

7. If you already pray the Rosary, share your experiences.

What benefits have come to you through the Rosary?

## *Let's Pray*

If you're not ready to pray the rosary, you can pray:

Holy Spirit, you guided our early Church fathers in the creation of the Apostles Creed and the development of the Hail Mary. You knew the weapons we would need against the enemy that threatens our capacity to love. Please help us to discern your will regarding these prayers and to embrace them with gratitude and joy for the gift. We ask all this in the power of the most Holy and Sacred Name of our Lord and Savior, Jesus Christ. Amen.

Otherwise, pick up your Rosary and pray one for those who might struggle with this particular chapter.

## *What's Next?*

You've almost reached the end of this book! Let's talk about what's next for you.

z

# CONCLUSION

## *Congratulations!*

You've completed all 23 sections and you've now got a better understanding of what the Catholic Church offers to help you get all the love, hope, and joy you could ever need all in one place.

I'm proud of you and I'm honored you've let me walk with you on this journey. But this is far from the end of your journey. It's just getting started.

So much more lies ahead of you. Let's talk about what comes next.

### Keep Studying

The Church is a mystery no less than any of the mysteries of the Rosary. She contains profound truths it will take you an eternity to unpack and fully comprehend. Not to mention 2,000 years of history of her own on top of all her inherited learnings from the Jewish faith. Don't expect to learn it all in a lifetime.

### Keep Praying

Prayers keep you connected to the ultimate source of love. They will help you grow in love, hope, and joy. Your prayers also act as a dial on a radio does. They help tune your mind into the things you want most in life, giving you greater clarity and wisdom about the best way to approach things.

## *Join the Community of Believers*

You can experience love anywhere, but you'll never get better opportunities to grow in love than in the community of believers. Get active, get involved, and contribute your time, money, and talent.

## *Attend Mass Regularly*

Remember, Jesus is at the altar waiting for you to arrive. He wants to give all of Himself to you, but you need to be there to receive it.

## *Join the Local RCIA or OCIA program at your parish*

We don't do altar calls in the Catholic Church because we're not looking for a quickie relationship that starts strong and dies just as fast. The RCIA/OCIA program is like a courtship, where you and Jesus are getting to know one another before you decide to commit to an eternity of being together. Be patient with the time it takes and trust the process.

## *Share the Good News*

If you've gotten value out of this course and you think other people should take it, I encourage you to share. It's the best way that we can be sure more people are equipped with the tools needed to live lives of authentic love. The more love in our world, the better and healthier our world will become.

> *He said to them, "Go into all the world and preach the gospel to all creation." - Mark 16:15*

If you're not sure where to get started on that, visit https://lovingcatholicism.com/course/turning-problems-into-prophets and I'll walk you through the process in a free, self-paced online course.

Now that you know what to do next, let's do one final

round of exercises.

## *Exercises*

Journal your answers to the following questions:

1. Do you feel better equipped and empowered to share the Good News with others?

2. What will you do to ensure that others receive it?

3. Which of your talents and gifts will you employ to make sure that others receive the good news of God's love for them?

4. What parish do you belong to?

5. If you don't belong to a parish, what's the nearest Catholic Church to you?

## *Let's Pray*

Holy Spirit, you set the hearts of the apostles on fire for sharing the message of Christ's good news with the world. Please work in us to help set our hearts on fire so that we, too, can participate in your work of saving souls. We ask all this in the power of the most Holy and Sacred Name of our Lord and Savior, Jesus Christ. Amen.

# ABOUT THE AUTHOR: BRANDY M. MILLER

## From Fallen-Away Catholic to Passionate Catholic Revert

Award-winning author and international speaker, Brandy left the faith at age 16 after being unable to find the answers that could satisfy her from Catholics she knew - including a priest and a sister. She assumed there were no answers.

More than a decade later, her 7-year-old son not only threatened suicide but had a backup plan in case the first plan didn't work. She didn't know what she and her husband did to break their baby so badly that he preferred death to life, but she knew she had to find out - and fast.

That marked the beginning of a journey which led her back to the Catholic faith and to finding the answers she needed to put her doubts about Church teachings to rest. Now, she strives to share the Good News with everyone she meets and to make Christ as real and present for them as He is for her.

## Connect with Brandy Online

website:https://lovingcatholicism.com

email: brandy@lovingcatholicism.com

Twitter (X): @writerbrandy

LinkedIn: https://www.linkedin.com/in/brandymmiller